MATTHEW

VOLUME 1: CHAPTERS 1–7

Ryan R. Harder

ISBN 979-8-88644-224-3 (Paperback)
ISBN 979-8-88644-225-0 (Digital)

Copyright © 2023 Ryan R. Harder
All rights reserved
First Edition

All rights reserved. No part of this publication may be reproduced, distributed, or transmitted in any form or by any means, including photocopying, recording, or other electronic or mechanical methods without the prior written permission of the publisher. For permission requests, solicit the publisher via the address below.

Covenant Books
11661 Hwy 707
Murrells Inlet, SC 29576
www.covenantbooks.com

I did not write about Matthew 1:1–17. It is a genealogy, and I don't have much to say about it. As with anything written in this book, use it as you best see fit. (Titus 3:9)

(Day 1)

> Now the birth of Jesus Christ took place in this way. When his mother, Mary, had been betrothed to Joseph, before they came together, she was found to be with child from the Holy Spirit. And her husband, Joseph, being a just man and unwilling to put her to shame, resolved to divorce her quietly. (Matthew 1:18–19)

The name Jesus Christ is more than a name; it is a title. Referring to Jesus as *the* Christ is something to wrestle with, think about, and/or dwell on. Jesus was a real historical figure. This is not the argument, but referring to him as he truly is, Christ, is where discussions begin. Mary's abnormal/special/unique/other pregnancy would have caused numerous problems for her socially and personally. How would society respond to her? Would Joseph believe that Mary's pregnancy was from the Holy Spirit? At this point, Joseph was indeed planning to divorce Mary. The enemy was already at work, trying to cause discord between Joseph and Mary. This was not a peaceful and beautiful time for this young couple; it was a time of stress and discord.

Questions:

1. Who do you say Jesus is and how does that impact your daily life?

2. How is your time in the Word and why? Do you believe that The Bible is God's word?
3. How is your prayer life? Is it essential to your daily walk/ growth?

(Day 2)

> But as he considered these things, behold, an angel of the Lord appeared to him in a dream saying, "Joseph, son of David, do not fear to take Mary as your wife, for that which is conceived in her is from the Holy Spirit." (Matthew 1:20)

We see here that Joseph took time to consider these things—thankfully. This also points to the gravity of what is taking place here. An angel was sent to him; this was and is no ordinary birth. His decision, whether or not he knew it or not, would have an impact on the history of mankind. Joseph did have to act in faith in believing this angel, and that act of faith should not be taken lightly. The events surrounding the birth of Jesus Christ were and still are unique and special. This is a one-time event; hopefully we all respond in such a way that honors this incredible event. The angel directly tells Joseph to not fear, pointing out that this was indeed a fearful time for Joseph and Mary. They would be facing social pressure, family pressures, and personal pressures about faithfulness between one another. The text also explicitly tells us that he, Jesus Christ, *will* save his people from their sins. There are two imperatives here: We are sinners, and he will save us from our sins.

Questions:

1. Do you believe you're a sinner? Why or why not?
2. Hopefully, you will come to a place where you, like all of mankind, believe you are a sinner. How will you or do you respond to your sinful nature?
3. How do you respond in times of fear?

MATTHEW

(Day 3)

> She will bear a son, and you shall call his name Jesus, for he will save his people from their sins. (Matthew 1:21)

We read here what our savior Jesus Christ will do for his people. He will save every one of his people from their sins. There is no doubt in this verse; it does not say he might save his people, but he will save his people. Furthermore, there is also no room for doubt or confusion about his people being sinners. Jesus will save his people from their sins. The verse does not say he will save his people who have sinned and those that have not sinned. All of his people are the same; we are all sinners and need to be saved from our sins. Romans 3:23–24 states, "For all have sinned and fall short of the glory of God, and are justified by his grace as a gift, through the redemption that is in Jesus Christ." How can we possibly thank Jesus enough for deciding to come down from heaven to save his people from their sins?

Questions:

1. How else have you tried to be forgiven of your sins?
2. Do you believe there is another way to be saved from your sins?
3. Does the world teach us that we need to be saved from our sins? What does the world say about sin?

(Day 4)

> All this took place to fulfill what the Lord had spoken by the prophet: "Behold, the virgin shall conceive and bear a son, and they shall call his name Immanuel" (which means God with us). (Matthew 1:22–23)

We read here that this birth is a fulfillment of prophecy spoken of long ago (Isaiah 7:14). Again, this birth is other, the birth of Jesus Christ wasn't ordinary, do not treat it as such. Respond to this birth, consider the otherness of this life/eternal altering birth, think on it in a worthy manner. This birth is a life/eternal changing event and the impact is still felt over two thousand years later. Nothing else in your life has such eternal consequences as to when it comes to believing who Jesus is. There is no middle ground or easy decision to be made when it comes to Jesus Christ. Jesus is either the Christ, the son of God and the savior of mankind or he is not. He is either the man who can save your from your sins and make you right before the father or he is not. There is no fence to ride here when you come to a decision about Jesus Christ. Your decision, your decision that you can only make on your own, has eternal consequences. Luke 9:20, The he said to them, "But who do you say that I am? And Peter answered, "The Christ of God."

Questions:

1. What are some big decisions you have made in your life?
2. What decisions have you made in your life that have impacted you for years to come?
3. When was the last time you took time to consider who Jesus Christ is?

(Day 5)

> When Joseph woke from sleep, he did as the angel of the Lord commanded him: his took his wife, but knew her not until she had given birth to a son. And he called his name Jesus. (Matthew 1:24–25)

Joseph obediently followed God's command and married Mary. Yes, God does give us commands and expects/demands obedience and his commands won't always be easy. Thankfully, He is a mercy filled and grace filled God and is more than aware of our shortcomings, which has to do with Chris's birth. Even after obedience, life will still be difficult for Mary and Joseph. Mary is still pregnant before being married and Joseph did not impregnate her. Can you imagine telling that story to your family and strangers for the next 9 months? Being a follower of Christ does not guarantee ease of life. Having a baby out of wedlock then lead to a lot more difficulties than it does today. Do not take Joseph's and Mary's decision lightly. To choose to obey God's command was not light matter. Still today, to be a follower of the Triune God is no light, easy of flippant decision. Thankfully, those who have made that decision have the Holy Spirit living inside of them to help guide them.

Questions:

1. Where does your truth come from?
2. How do you respond to God's commands?
3. Is Jesus Christ still Jesus Christ during times of struggle?

(Day 6)

> Now after Jesus was born in Bethlehem of Judea in the days of Herod the king, behold, wise men from the east came to Jerusalem, saying, "Where is he who has been born king of the Jews? For we saw his star when it rose and have come to worship him." (Matthew 2:1–2)

These verses begin by pointing back to a specific time in history of when Jesus Christ was born. He was born during the time of King Herod. As I discussed earlier, the birth of a man, a carpenter, a son to Joseph and Mary, is not the crux of the argument surrounding Jesus Christ. The question facing mankind for over two thousand years now is, who is Jesus? Hopefully, your answer is or will be, he is the Christ! There is no greater question to wrestle with or chew on. The implications of who Jesus was/is, is eternal. Continuing with the uniqueness/otherness of Christ's birth, we now read about wise men coming to see him. They were actively seeking this *baby* out, a one-track mind devoted to finding/seeing this *baby* at a cost to themselves. They did not fly there, not even in coach, nor drive there; this trip would have been completed by camel or on foot. A key piece here is, why did they make this arduous journey? For the simple reason: to worship him, this baby who was born in a barn.

Questions:

1. Have you ever worked to see Jesus? How much effort have you put in to see Jesus?
2. What do you put effort into doing?
3. Who or what do you worship? What do you put effort into, like the effort we read about these wise men exerting?

(Day 7)

> When Herod the king heard this, he was troubled, and all Jerusalem with him; and assembling all the chief priests and scribes of the people, he inquired of them where the Christ was to be born. (Matthew 2:3–4)

We now have another example of how a man, a *king*, responded to this birth. King Herod's response was one of disturbance and all of Jerusalem with him. The birth of this *baby*, Jesus Christ, was taken very seriously by wise men, King Herod, and all of Jerusalem. This birth was not something they glazed over or took flippantly. In fact, King Herod's disturbance put him into action; he did not just move on or past this birth. Herod, *the king*, took time to assemble all the chief priests and scribes to learn more about this *baby*; these men would have been known as experts or professionals in this field. He was taking his own time and the time of others to investigate and learn more about Jesus. If you are familiar with this part of the story, you are well aware that Herod's actions are not noble or so that he too could go and worship. What you are hopefully seeing is that Jesus Christ's birth demands a response; it cannot simply be overlooked or shrugged off.

Questions:

1. Have you ever been disturbed by the birth of Jesus Christ? Why or why not? King Herod was troubled by his birth.
2. Who have you gone to for guidance to learn about Jesus?
3. What do you take enough interest in to seek out professional advice or opinions on?

(Day 8)

> They told him, "In Bethlehem of Judea, for so it is written by the prophet: "And you, O Bethlehem, in the land of Judah, are by no means least among the rulers of Judah; for from you shall come a ruler who will shepherd my people Israel." (Matthew 2:5–6)

Embarrassingly, numerous times I have simply glossed over Old Testament prophecy that is referenced in the New Testament. Once I was blessed in recognizing that Jesus is the Christ, accepting that I was (and still am) a sinner in need of saving, knowing that I was condemned by the Triune God to an eternity in Hell, and that only Christ's blood could cover me and make me right before God the Father, that was it. I am now continuing to learn how the Old Testament points to Jesus Christ as the one and only savior. This shouldn't be a surprise, as I will daily be getting to know the Triune God better as I read his Word and spend time in prayer. There are some books in the Old Testament that I greatly enjoy, and they are all inspired by God, but world and human history has never been a strength of mine. All that being said, it is incredible to see how Jesus Christ fulfilled prophecy through his earthly ministry. To be able to personally know the ruling Shepherd as my Lord and friend is truly overwhelming. Knowing that Jesus Christ walked, faced and defeated the same trials and temptations that I face is both comforting and humbling.

Questions:

1. What books in the Old Testament are your favorite and why?
2. If you aren't reading the Old Testament, why not?
3. What does your daily, weekly, monthly or yearly Bible reading routine look like?

(Day 9)

> Then Herod summoned the wise men secretly and ascertained from them what time the star had appeared. And he sent them to Bethlehem, saying, "Go and search diligently for the child, and when you have found him, bring me word, that I too may come and worship him." (Matthew 2:7–8)

Herod was not taking the birth of Jesus Christ lightly, which is something ever pre-Christian should learn from him and every Christian should remember. His intentions were not good, but at least he knew that Jesus was not ordinary baby. He was even hoping to trick the wise men into helping him. Herod was at the very least suspicious of who this baby, who Jesus was/is and what the implications were. He then continues to find out more information about Jesus. Ironically, Herod's thoughts are consumed about finding out who Jesus was/is, even if it is for evil purposes. Jesus demands a response trying to pretend that He doesn't exist is not an option. King Herod's request is that the wise men search *carefully*, not nonchalantly, seeking Jesus is priority number one. Herod's intentions are pure evil, which we will see in a few more verses, but he has made a decision and there is no middle ground when it comes to your belief about Jesus.

Questions:

1. How do you show your belief about Jesus?
2. What are things you search carefully for?
3. What do you devote yourself to?

(Day 10)

> After listening to the king, they went on their way. And behold, the star that they had seen when it rose went before them until it came to rest over the place where the child was. (Matthew 2:9)

Scripture is very clear here, they did listen to King Herod, but they did not agree to do anything for him. Simply ignoring the king would have been out of the question. They respectfully listened to him and then continued focused on their journey to find baby Jesus. We do not get to learn very much about these men just that they are known as wise men who are currently being driven by one purpose. God the Father is clearly involved in helping these wise men find his son. The star that they had seen is still clearly visible to them, the Father is still providing direction for them to ensure that they will find his son. This is still true today; the Triune God still gives us guidance in finding him. A star has never played any role in my journey of getting to know Jesus Christ, at least not to my knowledge, but there have been numerous people in my life who have helped to guide me. False guides and distractions still exist as well, so we must diligently stay in the Word, pray, and walk in the Spirit to recognize them.

Questions:

1. Who or what distracts you from getting to know Christ?
2. How do you avoid or defeat distractions?
3. Who or what is your most trusted guide?

(Day 11)

> When they saw the star, they rejoiced exceedingly with great joy. And going into the house, they saw the child with Mary his mother, and they fell down and worshiped him. Then, opening their treasures, they offered him gifts, gold and frankincense and myrrh. (Matthew 2:10–11)

Seeing the star that continues to lead them causes them to be overwhelmed with joy, because they knew it would lead them to Jesus Christ. Scripture says they rejoiced with great joy. That is a lot of happiness, not just rejoicing, not just rejoicing with joy, but rejoicing with great joy. They knew their journey, their goal was going to be reached, they would see the Christ! The wise men's first response when they see baby Jesus is to fall to their knees and worship him. There was no hesitation when they saw Jesus, the only Christ. There was no doubt in those wise men that he would bring glory to the Father and is the only savior for sinners. Jesus Christ, Immanuel, had finally arrived and they're blessed to be able to worship him in person. What gift do we bring to the giver of the gift of salvation, to the only Christ who frees us of our sins? What response is fit for the of the universe?

Questions:

1. When was the last time you fell to your knees to worship Jesus? What led you to this worship?
2. Where are you today in your belief in Jesus?

MATTHEW

3. What, if anything, is keeping you from falling down and worshiping Jesus as your Christ?

(Day 12)

> And being warned in a dream not to return to Herod, they departed to their own country by another way. Now when they had departed, behold, an angel of the Lord appeared to Joseph in a dream and said, "Rise, take the child and his mother and flee to Egypt, and remain there until I tell you, for Herod is about to search for the child, to destroy him." (Matthew 2:12–13)

We continue with the sad, tragic, and terrifying story about who Herod truly was. The wise men did not go and report anything to him. In fact they completely avoided him after a dream from God. Then we have another account of a dream, warning Mary and Joseph to get away from Herod. Herod was a liar, a wolf in sheep's clothing, at best. He was saying the right words, "so that I can go and worship him" (verse 8b), but his intentions were much darker. Matthew 7:15–16 is a good reference about who he was. I also want us to consider Mary and Joseph. They had already almost suffered a divorce, social pressures, family pressure. Mary gave birth in a barn, and now they were forced to flee. Christians will face challenges, contrary to what you may hear being spewed on TV and in some churches. The Bible is where we get the truth.

Questions:

1. Have you ever been taught that your life should be easy after coming to know Jesus Christ as your Lord and Savior? How does that teaching align with the Scripture?
2. How do your marriage challenges compare to Mary and Joseph's?

3. If you are not married yet, what can you learn about marriage from Mary and Joseph?

(Day 13)

> And he rose and took the child and his mother by night and departed to Egypt and remained there until the death of Herod. This was to fulfill what the Lord had spoken by the prophet, "Out of Egypt I called my son." (Matthew 2:14–15)

Here we see another example of obedience—and quick obedience at that. Furthermore, there was nothing easy about what Mary and Joseph were about to do. Not only did they have to flee with a baby, but they did it at night. Even today, traveling at night creates more difficulties, challenges, and hazards. I am sure Mary and Joseph would have liked to get a good night's sleep before they began their journey, especially Mary, but off they went. Obedience to our Father is always for our best, but that does not mean it is necessarily easy or comfortable. Think about the lives of Jesus's twelve apostles and the prophets of old if you believe that a life of following Jesus will be all health and wealth. We also read another account of fulfillment of prophecy (Hosea 11:1).

Questions:

1. Have you ever dropped everything to follow a command from God? If not, how do you think you would/should respond?
2. How would you feel about following a command from God that seemed dangerous, uncomfortable, or that your family/friends didn't support?
3. When witnessing to others, do you think it is important to encourage them to count the cost? Consider Matthew 7:24–27.

MATTHEW

(Day 14)

> Then Herod, when he saw that he had been tricked by the wise men, became furious, and he sent and killed all the male children in Bethlehem and in all that region who were two years old or under, according to the time that he had ascertained from the wise men. (Matthew 2:16)

If you have read the Bible, you are well aware of the many stories of death that are present. For me, this is one of the most memorable, tragic, scary and horrific accounts of death. Maybe because it follows the most important time in human history. The contrast of events is so stark. This is not a make believe story, this is part of human history. This is who Herod was. People may be able to hide who they are for a time, but the truth always comes out. The scripture is very clear here, this was a massacre, an indiscriminate and brutal slaughter of two year old and younger boys. Thankfully, Mary and Joseph were obedient and had fled. The birth of Jesus was not and still today is not an ordinary birth that can be ignored. The life and work of Jesus Christ demands a response and there is no neutral ground. I recommend two older books. One is More Than a Carpenter by Josh McDowell and the other is The Case for Christ by Lee Strobel.

Questions:

1. Have you ever been tricked by someone who confesses Jesus Christ as his/her Lord and Savior? What do you think the purpose of that is? They aren't tricking God.
2. Do you ever try to hide who you are from God?
3. Is it comforting or concerning knowing that God knows all your thoughts and still showers you with his grace and mercy?

(Day 15)

> Then was fulfilled what was spoken by the prophet Jeremiah: "A voice was heard in Ramah, weeping and loud lamentation, Rachel weeping for her children; she refused to be comforted, because they are no more." (Matthew 2:17–18)

With these verses we get a little glimpse of who our Triune God is. These verses remind me of Jesus response to the death of Lazarus. John 11:32–35, Now when Mary came to where Jesus was and saw him, she fell at his feet, saying to him, "Lord, if you had been here, my brother would not have died." When Jesus saw here weeping, and the Jews who had come with her also weeping, he was deeply moved in his spirit and greatly trouble. And he said, "Where have you laid him?" They said to him, "Lord, come and see." Jesus wept. Never believe that the Triune God does not weep for his children. Mary's response is very similar to my response and I imagine many others, if you would have been here, they would have not died. I can only imagine this is the daily response of any human facing the loss of a loved one in a tragedy, such as in the case of the numerous drug overdoses in the United States every single day. I do not know why such things happen, but they will until Jesus Christ returns at the perfect time for humanity. Come Lord Jesus come!

Questions:

1. Where do you turn in times of tragedy?
2. How do you respond in times of tragedy?
3. Is it okay to be angry in times of tragedy?

(Day 16)

> But when Herod died, behold, an angel of the Lord appeared in a dream to Joseph in Egypt, saying, "Rise, take the child and his mother and

MATTHEW

> go to the land of Israel, for those who sought the
> child's life are dead." (Matthew 2:19–20)

Herod is now dead and the others who had tried to kill Jesus. Even though Mary and Joseph have been entrusted to raise Jesus Christ, the Savior of mankind, life has still not been easy. Since Christ's birth, life has continued to move as it was. We just finished reading about the baby massacre. And now we see that Joseph and Mary have been having to protect Christ from assassins. It appears to me that they are a good example of 1 Corinthians 10:13, I recommend reading it. This is a verse that I have struggled with numerous times over the last fifteen years or so. In my weaker moments when my faith and trust in God is struggling I might even have suggested to God that I am being tempted beyond what I am able and he might want to check His notes on who I am. Joseph and Mary, the human parents of Jesus Christ, faced countless trials. Why should I be surprised when life gets a little rough? According to scripture, it appears I should be surprised and maybe a little nervous if life as a Christian is easy.

Questions:

1. How often have you recalled Biblical examples that have been preserved for us in scripture during your times of struggle?
2. How do you respond when you are tempted in whatever way God is trying to grow you?
3. Do you ask God to help you grow closer to Him, to know Him better? Have you ever thought you might not like what that could take? Growth can be painful.

(Day 17)

> And he rose and took the child and his mother
> and went to the land of Israel. (Matthew 2:21)

Mary and Joseph are on the move again, thankfully at this moment, it is not because they are fleeing. We also see another example of this couple's obedience. The scripture says he got up and they headed out, no questions asked. This kind of obedience is exemplary. For me, my obedience to God is not always so swift and without throwing a fit or possibly a tantrum like a small child. Not only did the leave Egypt, which would make sense as people have been trying to kill their son since birth, but they continued to trust the Lord and fled to Israel. Even amongst the trials of their lives together with a newborn child, they still are obedient even to the finest points. Joseph and Mary have literally been blessed, chosen, called, or tasked with raising the son of God and they still are facing fierce and constant trials. The trials have been continual since before they were even married. Not only is their obedience impressive, but so is their perseverance.

Questions:

1. How would you rate your ability to persevere during times or struggles and/or disappointments?
2. How are you doing when it comes to being obedient to God?
3. When was the last time you considered the struggles that Joseph and Mary faced in their marriage and in raising a child?

(Day 18)

> But when he heard that Archelaus was reigning over Judea in place of his father Herod, he was afraid to go there, and being warned in a dream, he withdrew to the district of Galilee. And he went and lived in a city called Nazareth, so what was spoken by the prophets might be fulfilled, that he would be called a Nazarene. (Matthew 2:22–23)

Off Mary and Joseph went again. I am going to consider this one to be fleeing. Herod's son was now ruler, and we again read about a warning Joseph received in a dream to withdraw. It is interesting and encouraging to me that even Joseph was still feeling fear. After all the divine help that he had seen and experienced, he was still not above wrestling with fear. I can't help but wonder about the relationship between being afraid and struggling with trusting God. Matthew 6:25–34 seems to speak to this. My intent is not to mock or question Joseph but to encourage us. If Joseph struggled with being fearful, it is probably reasonable that we become fearful from time to time. We still want to rise above being fearful through God's strength, but we should not beat ourselves up over such occasions.

Questions:

1. How do you handle or deal with fearful situations?
2. What is your response when you feel like you have failed and/or sinned?
3. Reminisce about a time when you felt comforted by God.

(Day 19)

> In those days John the Baptist came, preaching in the wilderness of Judea and saying, "Repent, because the kingdom of heaven is at hand." (Matthew 3:1–2)

John has arrived on the scene to play his role of leading people to Christ. He is preaching, which implies that we need to be learning. Like it or not, no matter our age, our relationship/knowing/maturity in Christ, it is a lifelong process. We have not arrived, no one has arrived. Repentance is a key foundational piece of the Christian's life. Repenting needs to lead to the changing of our ways, changing from living a life full of sin to a life that points others to Christ. Our lives should no longer display the works of the flesh, but the fruit of the Spirit (Galatians 5:19–22). Asking for forgiveness of sins is crucial, and we are indeed forgiven, but I believe most of us do ask for forgiveness. How often do we ask God to help change us? We live in a constant battle with our sinful flesh and need our Father's help daily, minute by minute (Romans 7:15–20).

Questions:

1. Do you believe you need to change or are you content to just ask for forgiveness?
2. How often do you take the time to listen to a preacher or teacher and do you believe it is an important part of your Christian life?
3. When was the last time you asked God for help in battling your sin?

(Day 20)

> For this is he who was spoken of by the prophet Isaiah when he said, "The voice of one crying in the wilderness: Prepare the way of the Lord; make his paths straight." (Matthew 3:3)

We again are seeing more fulfillment of prophecy. There are some great books out there that you might want to consider reading focusing on the prophet Isaiah. The scripture does not describe or paint a picture of a man simply preaching, but crying out. If someone is crying out it shows or implies that they are desperate for others to hear and head what they are saying. That is what John the Baptist is doing. Scripture paints a picture of a man that is not too concerned with his speaking style or grace in presenting the message, but one who is desperate to get his message out to as many people as possible in any way possible. If you are familiar with John's attire it should also add to the scene. There is basically a crazy looking/acting man desperately crying out to get his message across to all that want to hear. John the Baptist is another great biblical role model in how the Christian should live his or her life.

MATTHEW

Questions:

1. What do you cry out about?
2. Is there anything in your life that you are desperate to tell others about?
3. What are you preparing for or trying to encourage others to prepare for?

(Day 21)

> Now John wore a garment of camel's hare a leather belt around his waist, and his food was locusts and wild honey. (Matthew 3:4)

What was John wearing and eating? Camel-hair with a leather belt. I do not know a lot about camels or making clothes, but I am pretty confident that *a* camel-hair garment would not be all that comfortable. Do any of us wear clothing made of camel-hair? I feel safe suggesting that his belt was not a designer belt either. He was probably quite the sight. We might be able to get on board with eating honey, but count me out when it comes to eating locusts, I don't even really like putting them on a hook. John's life was not glamorous, he faced challenges too, which we will read more about in the future. Hint, it will get worse. John had a clear focus on what he wanted to accomplish and he did not appear to be worried with much else. He was not deterred by his circumstances of life or by how he was seen by others. John was clearly confident in his calling and determined to do his part in serving his Lord.

Questions:

1. What would your response be if Christ called you to live a life that looked like John's?
2. Do you think John would be invited to speak at a Christian leaders conference today?

3. What advice do you think some Christian leaders of today would give John?

(Day 22)

> Then Jerusalem and all Judea and all the region about the Jordan were going out to him, and they were baptized by him in the river Jordan, confessing their sins. (Matthew 3:5–6)

Confessing of sins and being baptized was a key component in John's preaching. Some of us get squeamish or flat out avoid any preaching/teaching that suggests we are sinners. I guess it's not popular in today's culture? Our truth comes from the Word of God, not from man. We are all sinners, period. All of mankind desperately needs Christ's blood to cover us, there is no other answer to our sin. If there was another way to be made right in the eyes of the Father then Christ would not have done what he did. Maybe take a look at John 14:6. Our truth comes from the Bible. It is clear that Jesus, John, or any of the heroes in scripture were not particularly concerned with what people thought of them when it came to preaching, teaching and sharing God's Word. Never forget, it is the Word of God that convicts and leads people to the cross, not man's cleverness.

Questions:

1. How much confidence do you have in the Bible and it being *the* compass for your life?
2. Where is your limit (clothing, food, housing, etc.) when it comes to serving the Triune God?
3. How do you think you do when it comes to handling peer pressure?

MATTHEW

(Day 23)

> When he saw many of the Pharisees and Sadducees coming to his baptism, he said to them, "Brood of vipers! Who warned you to flee from the coming wrath?" (Matthew 3:7)

John was directly speaking to the religious leaders of the time when he called them a brood of vipers. These were the people who thought they had arrived and would have been outraged and angered at being called such names. John did not say the wrath that might come or be careful of the possible coming wrath. He clearly and definitely spoke of the wrath to come. The wrath of God is another topic that many people, pastors included, like to try and avoid. We, as a culture, like to highlight the love of God and rightfully so, but *when* Jesus Christ returns, it will not be as a lamb but as a lion. Truth and love—you can't have one without the other. If you aren't being truthful with someone, particularly when it comes to salvation, how can you say you love them? Wrath/judgment is coming, whether or not we believe it. The only way to successfully flee this coming wrath is to admit that you are a sinner, acknowledge that Jesus is the Christ, he is Lord, he died, rose again, ask him for forgiveness, and invite him to be Lord of your life. There is no other way. Our truth comes from the Bible.

Questions:

1. What urgency does the coming wrath of God create in you?
2. Who should you blindly follow and why?
3. Once you become a Christian, and the Holy Spirit permanently indwells you, do you have the ability to know Christ as well as anyone else?

(Day 24)

> Bear fruit in keeping with repentance. And do not presume to say to yourselves, "We have Abraham as our father," for I tell you, God is able from these stones to raise up children for Abraham. (Matthew 3:8–9)

John has just referred to the religious leaders as a brood of vipers and then moves right into telling them that they need to act in a way that displays a repentant heart. Yes, we are forgiven, but our lives need to be changed. For me, I picture myself trampling on the blood of Christ when I fall into being led by my flesh as opposed to walking in the Spirit. I know I am forgiven, and that brings me peace, but I am fearful of taking the sacrifice of Christ lightly. My sins were paid for by the blood of Jesus Christ, that is not an act to take frivolously. Years ago I heard a pastor giving a sermon about Christians being out-bred by other religions. Christians are not bred, everyone has to make their own decision. It does not matter who your father is, the decision to be a follower of Jesus Christ in an individual decision. I am often reminded of that sermon when I read this verse. As a parent, I do like to believe that the pastor meant to say something along the lines that we need to be doing our best to walk as Christ walked to point our kids to Christ. The Great Commission starts in our homes. First Timothy chapter 3 speaks to this.

Questions:

1. Have you ever contemplated if you take the blood of Christ too lightly?
2. If you grew up in a Christian home, when did you move past your parents belief and make it your own?
3. What does displaying a repentant heart mean to you? What does it mean in the scriptures?

MATTHEW

(Day 25)

> Even now the axe is laid to the root of the trees. Every tree therefore that does not bear good fruit is cut down and thrown into the fire. (Matthew 3:10)

I read this verse as being the refining fire and not the everlasting punishing fire of hell. Hell is a very real place and it is an eternal place where some people will go after their time on earth is over. One of John's key themes or messages is repentance. The Holy Spirit convicts of us sin and leads us to repentance. We need to be obedient and sensitive to those convictions. We will not be perfect this side of heaven due to our battle with our flesh, but we need to be striving to be like Christ. Succumbing or our sins or quitting the battle with our flesh is not an option for a Christian. Living a repentant life should have a natural outcome of bearing good fruit. Good fruit defined by our Triune God not by any human. If we resist the leading or prodding of the Holy Spirit then our Heavenly Father will lovingly refine us with fire for a time. Furthermore, John taught us in the prior scriptures that it is fallacy to rely on some mystical birthright to save us. If someone lives an unrepentant life, not confessing ones sins to Jesus Christ and asking him into his or her life they will face eternal damnation no matter who their parents were.

Questions:

1. How sensitive are you to the Holy Spirit's convictions?
2. When was the last time you asked the Lord to reveal your sins to you?
3. What do you think about the truth of your need to be refined by the Triune God?

(Day 26)

> I baptize you with water for repentance, but the one who is coming after me is more powerful than I. I am not worthy to remove his sandal. He himself will baptize you with the Holy Spirit and fire. His winnowing shovel is in his hand, and he will clear his threshing floor and gather his wheat into the barn. But the chaff he will burn with fire that never goes out. (Matthew 3:11–12)

The humility of John the Baptist is inspiring. Here is a man whose acts are worthy of being recorded and documented in our Holy Scriptures and what exemplary reverence he showed to Christ. John knew his role, his place, his gifting; there was not even a thought of trying to usurp Christ's place on the throne. He would model this continually in upcoming verses until his death, which was not pleasant. Jesus is still present even though he hasn't officially begun his ministry, which is why John's baptism was one of "only" repentance. His reference to Jesus's baptizing believers with the Holy Spirit is something that is still to come. This does not suggest that the present-day believer needs a "second baptism." The Holy Spirit does not come until after the ascension of Jesus Christ. That blessed, merciful, and gracious event has already happened in the present day but had not happened when John was speaking. Please consider taking a moment to read John 15:26–27 and 16:7–8.

Questions:

1. How does your humility compare to John the Baptist?
2. How does your reverence for Jesus Christ compare to John the Baptist?
3. If you are a follower of Jesus Christ, do you know and believe that the Holy Spirit has permanently indwelled you? How does that impact/encourage you both emotionally and effectively on a daily basis?

MATTHEW

(Day 27)

> Then Jesus came from Galilee to the Jordan to John, to be baptized by him. (Matthew 3:13)

What a truly amazing role model God gave us to follow. The humility Jesus shows us in submitting to the command of His Father, all believers are to be baptized, is humbling. He even goes to John instead of having John come to him. Christ willingly choosing to leave his rightful place in heaven, being separated from his Father for a time, and choosing to go to the cross to lay down his life, seems sufficient when it comes to obedience. He continuously shows displays his holiness with fulfilling every piece of the law. While Jesus is fully man and fully God, which our finite minds can't fully/completely grasp (please take a moment to read 2 Corinthians 5:7, and Deuteronomy 29:29), he never fails in modeling perfect obedience for us. If Christ himself takes the time to seek out baptism, we probably should too.

Questions:

1. What have you been taught about baptism?
2. Take a moment to remember and possibly share your baptism experience?
3. Take some time to marvel at and possibly discuss Christ's holiness

(Day 28)

> John would have prevented him, saying, "I need to be baptized by you, and do you come to me?" But Jesus answered him, "Let it be so now, for thus it is fitting for us to fulfill righteousness." Then he consented. (Matthew 3:14–15)

This is it, the ceremoniously beginning of our Lord and Savior coming to the forefront. Jesus Christ's earthly ministry is about to officially begin and humankind has never been the same since! What an exciting moment in the history of man, it is unbelievable and hard to comprehend what is taking place! We again see John's humility, he is in disbelief that he should be baptizing his Lord. John recognizes his need to be baptized by Jesus, he never once became prideful, thought that he had arrived, thought that he didn't need a savior or was equal to Christ. Furthermore, John is not worried about losing his power, or influence that he has gained in the eyes of others, like the Pharisees did. John has not become corrupted or driven by influence or power. His actions continue to show his character and back up what he said in verse 11.

Questions:

1. Please take a moment to dwell on the gravity of what is happening here, our Savior is about to reveal *the* hope, *the* peace, salvation!!
2. Who is your role model, earthly role model or other, and why?
3. Who are you an ambassador for, why (2 Corinthians 5:20)?

(Day 29)

> When Jesus was baptized, he went up immediately from the water. The heavens suddenly opened for him, and he saw the Spirit of God descending like a dove and coming down on him. And a voice from heaven said: "This is my beloved Son, with whom I am well-pleased. (Matthew 3:16–17)

This was quite the baptism, one only fit for a true king. There was nothing ordinary about his birth, and now we see that there was nothing ordinary about his baptism. The man, Jesus Christ, was no ordinary person, and to treat him as such is folly. To say there was a bit of a surprise as he came out of the water would be an understatement. The heavens were opened, the Spirit of God visually descended

MATTHEW

on him, and to cap it off, there was also an audible voice from heaven. This is a culmination as to what we read about in verses 13 to 15. Jesus's earthly ministry had officially started, and the announcement of his presence could not have been more clear, unique, and distinct. Many more miracles were yet to come, but what a proclamation to let mankind know that things would never be the same.

Questions:

1. In light of Jesus's baptism, how should we respond to baptisms that we actually get to see?
2. How does it make you feel that you can actively be a part of the ministry of Jesus Christ?
3. Do you believe that the Father loves you too, and you can please him? How can you please him?

(Day 30)

> Then Jesus was led up by the Spirit into the wilderness to be tempted by the devil. And after fasting forty days and forty nights, he was hungry. (Matthew 4:1–2)

Please do not miss who if leading Jesus into the wilderness. The Holy Spirit, a member of the trinity is the one who leads Christ, another member of the trinity to be tempted. Furthermore, his tempter is none other than the true enemy himself, the devil. This is not a temptation from the Pharisees, Sadducees, a lawyer or one with the spirit of the antichrist. The devil himself, he is real, comes to tempt Jesus Christ. If our true enemy is arrogant enough to think he can tempt our Savior, then we definitely need to always be on our guard. We also must not count on or depend on earthly weapons or defenses when it comes to the devil. Christians have to learn to fight with the sword of the Spirit, which is the word of God and learn to walk in the Spirit. Zechariah 4:6, Then he said to me, "This is the word of the Lord to Zerubbabel: Not by might, not by power, but by my Spirit, says the Lord of hosts.

Questions:

1. Do you believe in spiritual attacks?
2. Do you think the devil wants you to believe in spiritual attacks?
3. Why do you think the world scoffs at the idea of spiritual attacks?

(Day 31)

> And the tempter came and said to him, "If you are the son of God, command these stones to become loaves of bread." But he answered, "It is written, man shall not live on bread alone, but by every word that comes from the mouth of God." (Matthew 4:3–4)

This is the first of the devil's temptations of Jesus, but not the last. Satan will also continually send his minions to harass Christ throughout his earthly ministry. Although, he knows he is defeated, he does not stop attacking Christians. 1 Peter 5:8, Be sober-minded; by watchful. Your adversary the devil prowls around like a roaring lion, seeking someone to devour. He is looking to kill us, to silence us. The Pharisees took this same approach. The Bible does not tell us to live in fear, in fact the Word says just the opposite, but we must not be naive. I don't know how you handle hunger, but it is generally accepted that when people are hungry they are not at their best. We read here that Jesus had just fasted for forty days and forty nights, remember he is fully man and fully God, he does feel hunger. In this moment when Jesus is not at his best, when he is weak, that is when the enemy strikes. Let that be a lesson for us.

Questions:

1. If you are a Christian, do you believe that Satan is out to stop you from being an ambassador for Jesus Christ?

2. When you are feeling tempted, however that looks for you, do you recite scripture, go to prayer, or read the Bible?
3. What is your practice/discipline with fasting?

(Day 32)

> Then the devil took him to the holy city and set him on the pinnacle of the temple and said to him, "If you are the son of God, throw yourself down, for it is written, He will command his angels concerning you, and On their hands they will bear you up, lest you strike your foot against a stone." (Matthew 4:5–6)

Here we read about Jesus' second temptation from the devil. We again see the devil's boldness, arrogance, & pride, he actually quotes scripture to the Son of God! Have no doubt, our enemy does know the scripture, he is a fallen angel, he is not above twisting and/or manipulating the Word to try and trick us. Remember what happened to Adam and Eve. Tactics like this are still used today, it is not a new strategy. This style of attack can happen anywhere, even in places you might not expect. 2 Timothy 4:3–5, For the time is coming when people will not endure sound teaching, but having itching ears they will accumulate for themselves teachers to suit their own passions, and will turn away from listening to the truth and wander off into myths. As for you, always be sober minded, endure suffering, do the work of an evangelist, fulfill your ministry.

Questions:

1. What is your practice/discipline with reading the Bible?
2. Do you truly believe that you are in a battle (not a war)?
3. Do you believe that you have a ministry?

(Day 33)

> Jesus said to him, "Again it is written, "You shall not put the Lord your God to the test." (Matthew 4:7)

Our Lord and Savior does not flinch in bringing scripture to bare on his little adversary. Christ is not nervous, concerned or scared by the continued attack from the devil. Jesus is Lord and God. Maybe a little encouragement can be found in the following verse. Peter 5:9, Resist him, firm in your faith, knowing that the same kind of suffering are being experienced by your brotherhood throughout the world. Contrary to what the world wants us to believe, we are not alone. There are fellow Christians fighting the same battle we are fighting worldwide. The family of Christ is a big family, the brotherhood is not small and it has stood and will continue to stand the test of time. Christ is our cornerstone and there is no stronger cornerstone to be found or founded on. We *must* be in the Word, we *must* know the Word, which is knowing God, so that we will not be deceived (2 Peter 2:1–3, Matthew 24:11).

Questions:

1. Is it our responsibility to know the scriptures, know God, be in step with the Holy Spirit (Galatians 5:25)?
2. Take some time and discuss or think on how much fellowship there is globally for Christians. You are not alone.
3. How is your confidence in standing on the cornerstone of Christ?

(Day 34)

> Again, the devil took him to a very high mountain and showed him all the kingdoms of the world and their glory. And he said to him, "All these I will give you, if you will fall down and worship me." (Matthew 4:8–9)

MATTHEW

We should be getting a pretty clear picture of the relentless and continual attack our enemy brings upon us. This is the third and final temptation we read about where the devil himself tempts Jesus. We see here that the kingdoms of the world and their splendor are currently the devil's, but it is for a short time that we will have to stand against him. I can understand thinking a lifetime, eighty to one hundred years or less, is not a short time. If we keep in mind the eternal resting place that is waiting, keeping our eyes on heaven, then it is a short time that we spend in Satan's kingdom. The enemy's time will come to an end and then he will be cast into hell for an eternity. He will not escape punishment. There is never a time that we should feel merciful towards the devil, but it does appear that he has come to appoint of begging for Christ to worship him. He has used his biggest guns and they have not even left a scratch.

Questions:

1. How much effort do you put into resisting the devil, or the temptation to sin?
2. How often do you think about the splendor and magnificence of Heaven? How does it compare to your view of earth?
3. Do you ever have that feeling of "not again" when it comes to the temptations of devil?

(Day 35)

> Then Jesus said to him, "Be gone, Satan! For it is written, "You shall worship the Lord your God and him only shall you serve." Then the devil left him, and behold, angels came and were ministering to him. (Matthew 4:10–11)

In this case we see Jesus very simply and straightforwardly telling the devil to go away. He barely gave him the time of time. He was simply shooed away. He gave us another example to follow, which we can see James also referring to in James 4:7. Jesus resisted the devil and we can too through the power of the Holy Spirit. We also see Christ again quoting scripture and pretty much giving us a preview of the greatest commandment (Matthew 22:37). I also want to point out during each temptation Christ defeats the devil solely with the breath of his mouth, there is no real struggle, conflict or battle. Jesus speaks and it is all over (2 Thessalonians 2:8). Satan is less than a simple amoeba in comparison the one and only true Lord. There seems to be a lot of confusion about this in cartoons and elsewhere. This is not a fair or equal "fight," Jesus speaks and it is over. What does the final battle look like (Revelation 20:7–9)?

Questions:

1. Have you ever been taught or told that the devil and Jesus are equals, what does the Bible say?
2. Has it ever been taught or suggested to you that the devil rules hell? What does the Bible say (Revelation 20:10)?
3. What does worship the Lord your God and serving him only look like, how do you live that out?

(Day 36)

> Now when he heard that John had been arrested,
> he withdrew into Galilee. (Matthew 4:12)

I have tried to draw attention to the fact that many of God's people, heroes of the Bible, which John the Baptist is, faced many struggles, challenges and hardships. John has now been arrested and not because he is a criminal, but because he is doing his part to help people come to know Jesus as the Christ. Take a quick glance (or long glance) at 1 Peter 4:12–16 to get some further insight about suffering as a follower of Christ. Of course there is also the story of Job, which I assume we are all familiar with. Also of note is that Jesus withdrew into Galilee. Jesus did move around for a variety of reasons, he was not complacent. Jesus was not stationary, he actively sought out people and his goal of serving people required work and effort on his part. Scripture is also pointing to a change, John has been arrested and Jesus continues to move to the forefront.

Questions:

1. Hopefully you have not faced jail time, but have you ever been chastised for suffering?
2. Has suffering ever brought into doubt your standing with Christ?
3. In light of what scripture says, or remembering what scripture says, how do you think you should respond to the health and wealth message that is being preached?

(Day 37)

> And leaving Nazareth he went and lived in Capernaum by the sea, in the territory of Zebulun and Naphtali, so that what was spoken by the prophet Isaiah might be fulfilled: (Matthew 4:13–14)

For Jesus to move is obviously different than for many of us moving our families around for purposes or other reasons. It is rare for a pastor to stay in one church for his entire life or for a missionary family to stay in one place and change can be difficult. Matthew 8:20, And Jesus said to him, "Foxes have holes, and birds of the air have nests, but the son of many has nowhere to lay his head." That verse comes from the context of counting the cost of being a disciple of Jesus. Jesus is recognizing or validating that to not have a home is a trial or a cost. Hebrews 5:15, For we do not have a high priest who is unable to sympathize with our weaknesses, but one who in every respect has been tempted as we are, yet without sin. John the Baptist has just been arrested and Jesus is moving, again. The life of a Christian will have challenges.

Questions:

1. Take time to discuss or think about how much Jesus worked or how active he was.
2. What sins have you been challenged with when facing the cost of Christianity?
3. What do you think would be the most challenging move for you or what move would give you pause? What do you think Jesus's hardest move was?

(Day 38)

> "The land of Zebulun and the land of Naphtali, the way of the sea, beyond the Jordan, Galilee of the Gentiles-the people dwelling in the darkness have seen a great light, and for those dwelling in the region and shadow of death, on them a light has dawned." (Matthew 4:15–16)

In case there is any confusion about where Jesus was moving to or where he was willing to move to, scripture makes it clear that it was not to an extravagant resort. He moved toward the people who were living in the darkness, to those dwelling in the region and shadow of death. Jesus was never afraid to face challenges or to take the darkness head on. Christ did not schedule a vacation and then pretend it was a mission trip. Do not get me wrong, we must always be ready to preach the word, but Jesus never mislead anyone with what he was doing. He was never trying to impress anyone with his works or sacrifices, he was simply about living to bring glory to the Father. Jesus Christ brought a great, scripture does not say everyone wanted the light or accepted the light, but he brought it. We also have that privilege and command, bring the light while leaving the results our Triune God.

MATTHEW

Questions:

1. Where do you usually seek out people?
2. Where did Jesus seek you or where did he seek you out of?
3. How long did it take you to go with Jesus, to leave with him from where he sought you?

(Day 39)

> From that time Jesus began to preach, saying, "Repent, for the kingdom of heaven is at hand."
> (Matthew 4:17)

There can never be enough preaching or teaching about the importance, the criticalness of repentance. Teaching and preaching about repentance needs to saturate the land. Teaching and preaching about the need to repent, that works for salvation does not exist and that there is nothing that Christ's blood cannot forgive you of. Paul described himself as the chief of sinners, and God seemed to be able to find a way to use him for the glory of the Father. We are all active sinners who need to repent until Christ's return. Our sinful nature does not surprise our one and only Savior Jesus Christ. Jesus Christ willing chose to leave the presence of his Father, to be mocked, tormented, tortured and brutally murdering on a cross to lead us to repentance! Never forget what happened three days after his brutal killing on the cross. The cross is victory! We must be repentant people, people who accept/recognize the need for a savior and to then live in that repentance.

Questions:

1. When was the last time you repented?
2. When was the last time you should have taken the time to repent?
3. When was the last time you prayed that our Triune God would lead someone to repentance?

(Day 40)

> While walking by the sea of Galilee, he saw two brothers, Simon (who is called Peter) and Andrew his brother, casting a net into the sea, for they were fishermen. (Matthew 4:18)

What an amazing scene we see here while Jesus was simply out for a walk. Do not ignore the importance or simplicity of Jesus being out. The walk in and of itself is not grand, but he did make himself available. His availability led to the changing of two men for eternity! I am aware that there is more going on than we can see or understand, but it starts with going. You cannot be going and doing if you do not leave your house. I am willing to bet that Peter and Andrew had no idea that their lives were going to be changed that day at a moment's notice. I bet if someone would have told them that they would drop everything they knew, how they made their living, and their investment in a heartbeat to follow a stranger, they would have called them a liar. Jesus simply comes strolling by and they are changed for eternity, not just for their lifetime, but for eternity.

Questions:

1. Does the thought of going cause you anxiety?
2. If you are a Christian, do you know and believe that you are part of the Triune God's redemptive plan?
3. What part of going causes you the most hesitation?

(Day 41)

> And he said to them, "Follow me, and I will make you fishers of men. Immediately they left their nets and followed him. (Matthew 4:19–20)

Peter (Simon) and Andrew's response to the Savior is remarkable, simplistic and somewhat humbling. They did not hesitate, make any excuses about not being able to leave their jobs, leave their equipment or ask to hear Jesus's plan before going, they simply began following him. Do not gloss over or miss the blessed invitation that Jesus gave these simple plain men. These men were not elite, they were hard workers, but that is where the exceptionalism ends. This is the same thing he says to us, follow me. I am not suggesting that we have the same gifts, calling, or ministry as Peter and Andrew, I do not know, but we do have the same invitation, follow me. Sometimes we get caught up in so many hypothetical situations, or what ifs, which lead to the sin of worrying or fear, instead of simply following. God is very patient with us, we just need to get going on the journey he has planned for us and he will continue to refine us as we go with him. Psalm 34:8, Oh, taste and see that the Lord is good! Blessed is the man who takes refuge in him!

Questions:

1. When was the last time you took off on a journey of following the Savior?
2. Please take some time to discuss or dwell on God's blessed invitation to follow him.
3. What is it you think needs to fall in to place for your to follow him?

(Day 42)

> Going on from there, he saw two other brothers, James the son of Zebedee, and his brother John. They were in a boat with Zebedee their father, preparing their nets, and he called them. Immediately they left the boat and their father and followed him. (Matthew 4:21–22)

Once again, we see a quick and decisive response to the call that Jesus presents. We have brothers again that were fishermen, common men, not elite by any definition, and without any special training or skills *at this point*. There was nothing special about any of these men or any of the other men we would see, making up his twelve disciples. What is special is that they would have a three-year long course of a serious hands-on mentorship. This response is a little different in that these brothers left their dad in the boat by himself to go follow Christ. There is no reason to try and romanticize or justify what they just did to their dad. The Scripture clearly says, they left the boat and their father to immediately follow Jesus. Immediately.

Questions:

1. I would say the anti has been raised a bit here. How would you feel about leaving your father?
2. An argument could be made here that they were leaving their family business. Have you ever had to leave a family business or family to help with the Great Commission? How was/is that experience? If not, how do you think that would go?
3. How much do you think you would learn if you literally walked and lived twenty-four hours a day, seven days a week for three years with Christ?

(Day 43)

> Now Jesus began to go all over Galilee, teaching in their synagogues, preaching the good news of the kingdom, and healing every disease and sickness among the people. (Matthew 4:23)

The first thing I want to point out in this verse is that Jesus was going/doing; he was not sitting and waiting around. Jesus was busy teaching, which implies that we should be learners. If it was important enough for Jesus to be teaching, it should be clear that we need to be learning and growing. He was also preaching, which is different from teaching, but also strongly suggests that followers of Christ should be learners. I think of teaching as more of a back-and-forth time, like in a classroom. But preaching is more or a presentation where there isn't as much back-and-forth. We also see that Jesus has power over all illnesses, in case there was/is any confusion. Jesus's sole mission was not to heal people physically, although we do read in numerous places in the Bible about him doing so. His mission was to make disciples of all nations, which is what he charged us to do (Matthew 28:16–20).

Questions:

1. How much time do you spend in the Word, on a regular basis, getting to know Jesus, learning more about him, so you can reveal him to others?
2. Do you think it's important for Christians to be known as learners? Why or why not?
3. Does it excite you to know that you can be part of the Great Commission, literally teaming up with God to make disciples?

(Day 44)

> Then the news spread about him throughout Syria. So they brought to him all those who were afflicted, those suffering from various diseases and intense pains, the demon-possessed, the epileptics, and the paralytics. And he healed them. Large crowds followed him from Galilee, the Decapolis, Jerusalem, Judea and beyond the Jordan. (Matthew 4:24–25)

Jesus's reputation is growing. People were responding to what he is saying and doing. People were bringing other people to him to heal them of all kinds of ailments. His healing was now moving into the spiritual realm. He is healing those possessed by demons. Jesus was not just displaying his authority over the physical realm but also over the spiritual. We will continue to read more about Jesus's authority over demons as we move through Matthew. People weren't just coming from all over, but they were also following him wherever he went. It is very clear that Jesus was not just another random person to be ignored but someone who people were responding to. There was something unique about Jesus, and it is evident by how people were reacting to him.

Questions:

1. Do you think people then or now would be "experts" in Jesus's actions/activities?
2. Why do you think there is *still* so much debate about Jesus?
3. What do you think about healing the demon possessed? What are the implications of that?

(Day 45)

> Seeing the crowds, he went up on the mountain,
> and when he sat down, his disciples came to him.
> (Matthew 5:1)

This section of scripture is where we find some of the most famous or well-known teachings of Jesus. I want to point out, and will continue to point out in the future, that Jesus is constantly out with the people. He is also engaged with the people, he doesn't go to a public spot and pull out a book or some piece of technology, which presents an unapproachable persona. He actively seeks out conversation, and makes it very apparent that he is there to be with the people. The scripture tells us that Christ sees the crowds, he sees the people. Jesus is about people. He never says seeing people or being about people will be easy, but it is what he is about. I want to suggest that he still sets up a scenario where the people need to make a move towards him. Scripture tells us he sits down, he is available, but his disciples still need to come to him.

MATTHEW

Questions:

1. Would you describe yourself as someone who is our more or someone who is in more? Remember, being out does not have to be big and extravagant.
2. When you are out are you available, or are you just trying to check off a box of being out?
3. Do you see people?

(Day 46)

> And he opened his mouth and taught them, saying: "Blessed are the poor in spirit, for theirs is the kingdom of heaven. (Matthew 5:2–3)

What is Jesus doing here? Teaching! In fact, he goes up on a mountain and makes himself comfortable, waits for his disciples all for the purpose of teaching. He has purposely setup a teaching environment one might even call it a classroom. Poor in spirit means we know that we need something other or greater than ourselves, we need a savior. You could also think of it as knowing or recognizing our fallen state. Accepting this truth about oneself will lead to being welcome into heaven. Being poor in spirit might not be a shirt you want to wear or a shirt that others would buy. A shirt that says on the way to the kingdom of heaven would probably work, more people would say they want that, at least initially. One of the keys to entering that kingdom is being poor in spirit.

Questions:

1. How would you describe yourself, do you like crowds or small groups? Either way, hopefully you find a setting that works for you to share/discuss Christ and the marvels of His coming kingdom.

2. What thoughts or emotions do you have about engaging in conversations about Christ and/or God honoring conversations based on Biblical truths?
3. Please take a moment to read Proverbs 27:17 & 1 Corinthians 15:33. How do these verses apply to and/or guide conversations that we seek?

(Day 47)

> Blessed are those who mourn, for they will be comforted. (Matthew 5:4)

My first instinct when I begin to mourn is not a feeling of being blessed, but it is another area of my life that I am working on. I do turn to God, but it may take a few "conversations" until I am conversing with him in a correct manner. Where we turn or who we turn to and how that conversation looks say a lot about our faith/trust/confidence in God. God does lead me to a place of comfort or peace, but it takes me too long to get there. This can be an up-and-down situation for me the longer the mourning lasts. I encourage you to read some of King David's psalms during your times of mourning; you would be in good company (Acts 13:22). David and God had numerous honest conversations. Your emotions are real. God already knows them and can handle them. The smiles we wear during our times of distress/mourning will most likely trick people, but God knows the heart (Psalm 44:21).

Questions:

1. What is your first instinct when you start to mourn?
2. Do you have a person you can turn to during these moments or seasons that helps to direct you to God? If not, maybe consider making that a goal.
3. Please take a moment to meditate on the truth that God loves you even though he knows the failures we have and will have in the future while battling our flesh (1 Chronicles 16:34; Ephesians 1:13).

MATTHEW

(Day 48)

> Blessed are the humble, for they will inherit the earth. (Matthew 5:5)

Humility is a character trait that is not as highly esteemed by man as it is by God. In fact we regularly see the opposite on television, in magazines, in movies, and on numerous other technology devices. God has called us to something different—again/still, a character trait that goes against the norm. He doesn't tell us that it will be easy to live a humble life, but he does say that the humble will inherit the earth. I don't envy our kids and youth. Lack of humility is displayed in so many different ways now. Growing up, I remember only having to worry about having the right clothes and shoes. I never had to worry about having the right phone, tablet, or whatever new gizmo comes out seemingly on a daily basis. Living a humble or simple life seems to be getting trickier every day too.

Questions:

1. Do you enjoy being around humble people or proud overbearing people?
2. How do you display humility to others (kids, friends, coworkers)?
3. What does the balance of confidence, being proud of one's work, accomplishments, and humility look like?

(Day 49)

> Blessed are those who hunger and thirst for righteousness, for they will be filled. (Matthew 5:6)

To hunger and thirst for righteousness is such vivid language. It makes me think of craving after a delicious bacon cheeseburger, a big steak with buttery mashed potatoes, or a milkshake at my favorite ice-cream shop. I am challenged to consider my hunger and thirst for *righteousness*, to be seen as right before my heavenly Father. Thankfully, due to the work of my Savior, Jesus Christ, God sees him standing in my place. That being said, I do want to thirst and hunger daily to actually have righteous behavior so that I can reveal Christ to others. This is not a salvation issue. My salvation is secure. I have been sealed. this is an obedience issue. This is one of those times that I recommend taking a few minutes to read 1 John 2:3–6. We, followers of Christ, which is who I am, are told to walk just as he walked. I will fail on a daily basis then repent and constantly remember that I am loved and forgiven by God, but I will continue to hunger and thirst for righteousness to hopefully bring glory to God until I am called home.

Questions:

1. What do you hunger and thirst for?
2. How does hungering and thirsting for righteousness look during your day?
3. What do you think you will be filled with?

(Day 50)

> Blessed are the merciful, for they will be shown mercy. (Matthew 5:7)

Sign me up for wanting, desiring, and needing mercy shown to me on a moment-by-moment basis. I am a sinner. Recognizing this truth is a key step on the road to salvation. Taking a moment to read Romans 3:23, the whole chapter or even the whole book for that matter, might be worth your time, but a quick review at this moment should suffice. The only reason I can commune with God is due to the merciful acts of Jesus Christ. If mercy is a character trait of God, it stands to reason that it should be a character trait of mine too. Vengeance is the Lord's, He will repay (Deuteronomy 32:35, Romans 12:19). This is a struggle of mine, especially when I feel like my kids or wife are being attacked, but I need to trust God and, more importantly, obey his commands. My understanding is that patience is also a virtue or maybe something bigger, such as a fruit of the Spirit. Patience is another area that God has not quit refining in me.

Questions:

1. Do you feel the need for mercy?
2. Is it easy or difficult for you to show mercy?
3. When was the last time you thanked God for his mercy that he covers you with?

(Day 51)

> Blessed are the pure in heart, for they will see God. (Matthew 5:8)

Where do we get or find this purity? How can we attain purity? I am going to use holy and righteous as synonyms for pure. All of these attributes or qualities are heart issues that we cannot attain on our own. A completely fallen being, which is what humans are, cannot attain purity on their own (Mark 7:21; Jeremiah 17:9). This is a truth that mankind has to accept, which is now seen as taboo to even teach/preach about in church, but it is in the Word of God, which is where we get our truth from. Our hearts need to be made new, and that can only happen through Christ's blood. Holiness, righteousness, and purity are defined by God, not by man. And in his eyes, we all fall short. Man will continue to try and redefine or move the bar when it comes to God's standards, but that is fallacy. We must be holy (1 Peter 1:16), pure, and that is only possible by the work of Jesus Christ.

Questions:

1. What do you think about trying to attain purity of the heart?
2. How do you feel about your depravity?

3. What teaching/preaching have you heard about needing to be pure/holy/righteous?

(Day 52)

> Blessed are the peacemakers for they will be called sons of God. (Matthew 5:9)

At one point in time, I remember this character trait seeming to be placed above all the others, which always confused me. For the record, I don't see anywhere in Scripture where it is suggested that Jesus had put them in an order of importance. Living a peaceful life is spoken about in other places of the Bible (1 Timothy 2:2), but this verse seems to point toward reconciliation, restoring peace. I am wondering if this is pointing to those who help create peace and reconciliation between God and man. This would tie directly into the Great Commission (Matthew 28:18–20). There is also no greater or more important peace that needs to be made, fostered, or shared than between God and man. Isn't our prime focus in life eternal peacemaking? Peacemaking between people is temporary, but peacemaking between God and man is eternal peacemaking. Creating peace between people is excellent, but don't forget our eternal calling.

Questions:

1. How much of your time do you commit to being a peacemaker between people?
2. How much of your time do you commit to being a peacemaker between God and man?
3. Assuming/hoping/praying that you have accepted Jesus Christ as your Lord and Savior, how much joy, gladness, thankfulness, and any other positive emotion arise in you when you dwell on the truth that you are a child of God?

MATTHEW

(Day 53)

> Blessed are those who are persecuted because of righteousness, for the kingdom of heaven is theirs. (Matthew 5:10)

Here is another truth of the Bible that is a little tough to stomach. Am I supposed to feel blessed when persecuted? My initial response and reaction is to avoid persecution. There is a key qualifier here though: because of righteousness. Well, we already discussed thirsting and hungering for righteousness. And if the outcome happens to be persecution, then that is a price I am more than willing to meet. Righteousness leads to being blessed, and persecution leads to being blessed too. Furthermore, the blessing comes from God and is eternal. My mind, eyes, and heart need to be focused on eternal things (2 Corinthians 4:18). This again flies in the face of the false teaching that comes from the health and wealth "teaching." Persecution is a natural outcome of living a righteous life (John 15:20). Keep your eyes on the prize (Philippians 3:14), and do your part to bring as many people with you. For the kingdom of heaven is theirs. There is literally no greater prize. Nothing that man can offer comes close, and that is a huge understatement.

Questions:

1. How much do you desire to be blessed by God?
2. How important to you is praise, admiration, accolades, and being noticed by people?
3. What scares or worries you the most when it comes to persecution?

(Day 54)

> You are blessed when they insult you and persecute you and falsely say every kind of evil against you because of me. Be glad and rejoice, because

your reward is great in heaven. For that is how they persecuted the prophets who were before you. (Matthew 5:11–12)

I find it interesting that this seems like an attachment to the final beatitude, which is the only beatitude that has anything like this. Lumping all three verses together seemed like an okay idea, but I think there is extra emphasis here from Jesus, so I thought I should separate them out. There is more added here, or more details, insults may lie in every kind of way against followers of Christ. That really leaves the door open, every kind of evil against you. There is still a qualifier here: because of me. People insulting, persecuting, and lying about you could be because you are not nice. I recently heard a sermon about this topic, and the pastor said, there are only two options: You are being persecuted because of your relationship with Christ, which means you are blessed, or you are acting like a jerk. When you face these actions, you are the only one who can honestly evaluate why it is happening. Seeking wise and honest counsel would also be good to make sure it's not just because you are mean. Telling us to be glad may sound a little strange, but remember, Jesus faced it all, and he is the only one who has ever walked earth, knowing how great heaven is. He knew what he was going to face and still, in his omniscient, says to be glad and rejoice because we will receive a great reward in heaven. I am going to trust his judgment. That doesn't mean we shouldn't show sympathy or possibly even empathy, depending on your life experiences, when someone is going through these trials. Remember, you are in good company *when* you face these times.

Questions:

1. How do you respond when people lie about you? Have you ever considered it could be due to your belief in Jesus?
2. Who do you go to for wise counsel? Who can you trust?
3. What do you envision when you consider being treated like the prophets who were before you?

MATTHEW

(Day 55)

> You are the salt of the earth. But if the salt should lose its taste, how can it be made salty? It's no longer good for anything but to be thrown out and trampled under people's feet. (Matthew 5:13)

This is a declarative statement by Jesus—a fact. You, me—we are the salt of the earth. It is interesting to me that he says Christ's followers are *the* salt, not some salt or a salt. We are meant and/or designed to bring truth to the world. Having no salt or losing our saltiness suggests that we aren't having an impact, aren't sharing the Word, aren't doing our part to bring others to Christ (1 Corinthians 3:6; Ephesians 2:10). If we are lacking salt in our life, then we simply look like everyone else, and we are called to be different. Our saltiness has a unique and special ingredient. We are special salt. We are not called to be overbearing or too strong (2 Timothy 2:24–25). Our saltiness requires tact, wisdom, knowledge, patience, and prayer. Most importantly, it takes trust and reliance on God. Did you catch that piece in 2 Timothy 2:25b? *Perhaps*, we might get to see someone accept Christ as their Lord and Savior, or it might come at another time, but we must remain salty and do our part in submission to our heavenly Father (2 Corinthians 2:14–17).

Questions:

1. Do you put yourself in positions to be salty and/or look for those opportunities?
2. Do you struggle with being too salty or not salty enough? Christians are a tricky recipe.
3. Have you ever struggled with thinking that you need to be the one to save someone? How do you feel about being part of the team but maybe not the lead piece or the piece that gets the accolades?

(Day 56)

> You are the light of the world. A city situated on a hill cannot be hidden. No one lights a lamp and puts it under a basket, but rather on a lampstand, and it gives light for all who are in the house. (Matthew 5:14–15)

These verses are right on the heels of Jesus, telling us that we, Christ's followers, are the salt of the earth. He is now comparing his followers to being a light—and a light to the whole world. Jesus is continuing to emphasize that we need to carry on his teaching and to live the way that he lived. This is no light calling and not a charge to be taken lightly. He continues here, telling us that we are not to hide our lamp or hide the message that Christ has given us to preach and teach. In fact, our lights are supposed to be easily seen, placed in an area for all to see. I think Matthew 17:1–9 speaks to this, which is where Jesus is transfigured right in front of them. Peter suggested setting up three shelters and staying there, but Jesus quickly had them up and moving again, going out to be salt and light. I would have liked to stay there too and others try to create such settings, but we are not called to stay in such places. Rest and relaxation are coming, but it is not here yet.

Questions:

1. How are some ways you can be a light?
2. Does "light work" have to be grand? Consider meaningful actions done for you, were they always or ever grand?
3. Consider the parable of the Good Samaritan. I know he is in Scripture, but how much praise, adoration, or glory did he get or seek for his "light work"? I don't think he would have taken a selfie or posted about it.

MATTHEW

(Day 57)

> In the same way, let your light shine before others, so that they may see your good works and give glory to your father in heaven. (Matthew 5:16)

What an indescribable gift it is that God has enabled us, completely fallen creatures, to somehow shine a God-honoring light in this dark world. We are described as lamps that shine the brightest bulb possible—the bulb of God. All of this light that we have been given the opportunity to shine solely comes from God; there was no light in us. Never forget the fall and who completely we all were before the mercy and grace of Jesus Christ's sacrifice. Do not let the truth of being a lamp of light for God lead you to pride. God opposes the proud. All glory and praise belong to our Father in heaven. We are blessed beings in that we play an active part in the saving work of the one and only true God. It's pretty incredible when you take a moment to think about what we are a part of. I hope Christ's light blindingly shines out of me more and more each day.

Questions:

1. Please describe the last place you let your light shine.
2. How do you go about trying to make your light bulb shine brighter?
3. How do you fight off pride when you get to see and experience the work that Christ does through you?

(Day 58)

> Do not think that I have come to abolish the law or the Prophets; I have not come to abolish them but to fulfill them. (Matthew 5:17)

Jesus has indeed fulfilled the law, and we are saved by mercy and grace. But we have still been given a high calling—a higher calling than being under the law. We are no longer saved by the law, to be forgiven by following the law, or to be made righteous by following the law, but now we have the calling to reveal or show Christ to others by how we live, which is by humbly following the law by the power of the Holy Spirit. Our bar is to be Christlike, no exceptions. We will fail, be led to repentance on a continuing cycle, never arriving until we see Christ standing in our place before God our Father. We obey the law to help reveal Christ to others to the best of our abilities/gifts to do our part in fulfilling the Great Commission, never forgetting the unfathomable and undeserving gift that Christ gave us by going to the cross.

Questions:

1. Take a moment or two to think about what your life would be like if Jesus hadn't willingly chosen to leave heaven to bring glory to the Father, defeat sin, defeat death, and save sinners.
2. When was the last time you let yourself trust in the power of the Holy Spirit?
3. How do you deal with and handle failure?

(Day 59)

> For truly, I say to you, until heaven and earth pass away, not an iota, not a dot, will pass from the law until all is accomplished. (Matthew 5:18)

In case there was any confusion, God again clearly tells us with different words that nothing in the law will pass away. Until Christ makes his triumphal return—and I mean triumphal—nothing in the law will pass away. This hopefully leads us again to being thankful for the work that Jesus completed. When all is accomplished, people who are not covered by Christ's blood will be in for a very eye-opening, terrifying experience. Those who only highlight the suffering lamb part of who Christ is by ignoring the totality of Scripture will wish they took the blessed and available teaching of the Bible more seriously while they were alive. The seriousness of the truths that accompany the coming of the accomplishment of Christ's work should spur those of us who know Jesus Christ as Lord and Savior into action. Every Christ's follower needs to be getting with the going and doing. The second coming of Christ is a real thing that will happen.

Questions:

1. What emotions do you feel when you meet or think about those who don't know Jesus as the Christ?
2. When was the last time you took time to think about what it will look like when Christ returns as the conquering King?
3. Do you feel confident that you are doing all you can with the spiritual gift(s) that God has given you? Why or why not?

(Day 60)

> Therefore whoever relaxes one of the least of these commandments and teaches others to do the same will be called least in the kingdom of heaven, but whoever does them and teaches them will be called great in the kingdom of heaven. (Matthew 5:19)

I don't know exactly what it means to be called least in the kingdom of heaven, but I would like to avoid that title. This verse does make me think of James 3:1: Not many of you should become teachers, my brothers, for you know that we who teach will be judged with greater strictness. What pastors teach or don't teach does have consequences. Every Christian is called to know Christ more and more throughout our journey, but pastors are teachers of the Word of God. To seek to become a teacher of God's word should not be taken lightly, at least how I understand what Scripture is saying here and in James 3:1. A look at the books of Timothy and Titus also might be educational when it comes to declaring someone a pastor. It's my experience that numerous "pastors" have no training. People get trained to do all sorts of things; even driving large trucks takes a special license. I do not know how many times I have heard someone say, my pastor is nice and loves Jesus. Shouldn't that describe every Christian? We Christians are missing the mark when it comes to declaring someone a teacher of God's word, and there are consequences to that.

Questions:

1. What job has more lasting consequences than the handling of God's word?
2. Do you ever give second thought to how you teach God's truth to people or share what you know about Jesus? What can we do to try and not do this?
3. How do you feel when people misrepresent who you are or lie about you?

(Day 61)

> For I tell you, unless your righteousness exceeds
> that of the scribes and Pharisees you will never
> enter the kingdom of heaven. (Matthew 5:20)

A natural question arises: How can our righteousness exceed that of the scribes and Pharisees? First, Christ never complimented the scribes or Pharisees on their righteousness. The scribes and Pharisees received some of the greatest rebukes from Jesus that we read about in Scripture. The spiritual leaders knew the Scriptures; some had the Old Testament memorized. But when God in the flesh was in their midst, they didn't worship him; they led the people to crucify him. Scripture also tells us that not all of the spiritual leaders rejected

Jesus; some did come to recognize him as the Christ. Secondly, our righteousness comes from our Lord and Savior Jesus Christ. We can never obtain godly righteousness on our own. Every human on earth needs to humbly accept that they are a sinner and that we must be covered by Christ's blood to be seen as righteous before the one and only judge, God the Father. The pride of completely fallen, unregenerate mankind fights against this truth, but God's actions point us to the only truth, which is thankfully clearly recorded in the Bible.

Questions:

1. Since numerous spiritual leaders didn't recognize Jesus as the Christ, even though they knew the Scriptures, does that mean we shouldn't read the Scriptures? (Hint, the answer is no.) Why or why not?
2. When did you stop trying to earn righteousness on your own? Does that temptation ever return?
3. Why do you think it's a struggle to accept Jesus's righteousness?

(Day 62)

> You have heard that it was said to those of old,
> "You shall not murder; and whoever murders will
> be liable to judgment." (Matthew 5:21)

Jesus is continuing to make it clear that the law is not being removed, and we will soon see that he is actually upping the expectation. He is speaking to all mankind here. You shall not murder. There shouldn't be any confusion, even though it appears like there is plenty of confusion about committing murder. If someone does "get away" with murder, that doesn't mean it is okay in the real judge's courtroom. You shall not murder. Jesus goes on to say that if you do murder someone, then you will be liable to judgment. We see here again that Jesus is stating a plain fact. You will—not if—be liable to judgment. God's law did and still does trump man's laws. The judgment we face here on earth is not the final judgment that we'll face. No matter what country you're from, no matter how great you think your judicial system is, or how great or progressive mankind thinks it is or is becoming, we will never be able to circumvent God's laws.

Questions:

1. Do you think we struggle with convicting or deciding who is a murderer? Why or why not?
2. What does the Bible say about how we should punish those who commit murder?
3. Do you think it is a given today that all people have heard what is said in the Bible, let alone believe what it says? If not, why is that?

(Day 63)

> But I say to you that everyone who is angry with his brother will be liable to judgment; whoever insults his brother will be liable to the council; and whoever says, "You fool!" will be liable to the hell of fire. (Matthew 5:22)

This is a great example and reminder that Jesus is the Word. Christ Jesus isn't erasing Scripture, removing the law, or even relaxing any commandment. What he's doing is adding to it, making it more or making it clearer. There should be no question that we should not murder, but Jesus has called us to not even get close to murder. The standard he has set is for us to not even be angry with our brother. Scripture tells us, in our anger, we are not to sin, so we will wrestle with anger. When we become angry, don't let that anger turn to sin by directing it toward our brother. Bring our anger to Christ. We must stop blaming others for our sin. We need to take our sins to Jesus, asking for forgiveness, and repent. Jesus even tells us not to say you fool. The consequences of not obeying Jesus makes us liable to the hell of fire. Being obedient in dealing with our anger can only be done by humbly looking to Christ for strength.

Questions:

1. Is it difficult for you to rely on Christ for strength throughout the day?
2. How often do you blame someone else for the anger you are wrestling with?
3. Do you feel uncomfortable knowing that there are consequences for sin?

(Day 64)

> So if you are offering your gift at the altar and there remember that your brother has something against you, leave your gift there before the altar and go. First be reconciled to your brother, and then come and offer your gift. (Matthew 5:23–24)

Here we see Jesus emphasizing the importance of reconciliation. Gifts are good, but they are also external, where matters of the heart (reconciliation) are internal and can be harder to practice. I heard a great sermon from a pastor a few years ago. He did an excellent job explaining the difference between forgiving others and reconciliation. I had never heard a sermon like it before and haven't heard one like it since. Forgiveness is a command. Matthew 18:21–22 is one place you can find this command clearly discussed between Jesus and Peter. Forgiving others is not an option. We are to forgive others just as God has forgiven us, and it is an action we can do on our own. Reconciliation is much trickier because it involves at least two people. We cannot control other people, nor force them to reconcile; that is the Holy Spirits job. How many messes have Christians created by trying to force/coerce others to repent before the Holy Spirit has done that work in them? In Romans 12:18, we read that, if possible, as far as it depends on you, live at peace with everyone. We may be ready to reconcile, but the other person may not be ready. Go and be ready to reconcile. That depends on you, but the Holy Spirit may still be working in the other person's heart.

Questions:

1. What is an external sin that you need to confess to God and ask his help in repenting from?
2. What is an internal sin that you need to confess to God and ask his help in repenting from?
3. What sins are easy for you to repent of?

(Day 65)

> Come to terms quickly with your accuser while you are going with him to court, lest your accuser hand you over to the judge and the judge to the guard, and you be put into prison. (Matthew 5:25)

The key point here is to come to terms quickly with your accuser, work to be in the right relation with all people. Jesus gives us an example here of having to go all the way to court and possibly even to prison. All broken relationships aren't this severe, but the main focus of this verse is to come to terms quickly with your accuser. This does not mean you need to concede to a lie or become part of a lie to live at peace with everyone (Romans 12:18). Jesus never calls us to concede to sin, accept false teaching, or to join in sinful actions by others to live at peace. Jesus Christ was a staunch defender of the truth and never compromised when it came to Scripture. Are the other hurts or grievances that we can and should let go of to live at peace? The answer is clearly yes. Jesus accepted all kinds of wrongs said and done to him but not when it came to biblical commands. He went to death defending the truth, along with many other biblical heroes, and Christians are still being put to death, defending the

MATTHEW

truth in our time. There are many documented heroes of the Bible that did indeed go to prison defending the truth, and this is still occurring today. The wholeness of the Bible teaches us to come to terms quickly with your accuser and to live at peace with everyone, but never does it teach to compromise (lie) about biblical truths.

Questions:

1. Discuss or think about times when you have had to make difficult relationship decisions based on biblical truths.
2. Has your faith in the triune God been tested yet to the point of having to go to court? How did you respond, or how do you think you would respond?
3. Have you ever faced prison due to your faith in Jesus Christ? How did you respond, or how do you think you would respond?

(Day 66)

> Truly, I say to you, you will never get out until you have paid the last penny. (Matthew 5:26)

This is the last verse in this section where Jesus is talking about anger. His examples here have led us all the way to dealing with our anger, possibly leading us to court and even prison. We must deal with our anger in a God-honoring way, and that means bringing it to our Savior and leaning on him when we are in danger of letting anger lead us to sin. This verse also points us to thinking about what sin leads us to, needing to pay to the very last penny if we rely on the law to save us. Sin leads us to death, and the only way to have our sin paid for is to put our faith in the saving work of Jesus Christ; that is the only way our debt can be paid. Never forget how great our debt to be paid is. It took Christ Jesus's sacrifice to pay off our sin debt so that we could be in relationship to the Father. Every "little" sin—man is the only one that would ever describe any sin as little—

separates us from our Father. Christ made the payment that was due for our sins to the very last penny.

Questions:

1. I have lots of school debt, so the idea of debt is very tangible to me. How often do you think of your sin as a debt that needed to be paid for?
2. This verse also makes me think of bail that is needed to be paid to get someone out of prison. What was our bail to get out of hell?
3. How many times did that payment need to be made to pay for each and every one of our sins in full from birth to death (John 19:28–30)?

(Day 67)

> You have heard that it was said, "You shall not commit adultery." But I say to you that everyone who looks at a woman with lustful intent has already committed adultery with her in his heart. (Matthew 5:27–28)

Here again, we read that Jesus is not abolishing the law but has raised the expectations or defined more clearly what it means to commit adultery. You may have heard or even been told by someone you love that it is okay to "look," but that is not what God has taught us. This is another example of an internal sin. It is easier to hide an internal sin, but it still separates us from our Father. The world (man) will tell you otherwise and show you otherwise through television, movies, streaming services, and walking down school hallways. Mankind will also try to get you to go along into sin, but man is not the Judge, and man does not change Scripture. We will fail and sin on a daily basis or even more frequently than that, but we cannot let our failures lead us to trying to justify our sin. We must call a sin a sin according to the Word of God and humbly be led to repentance.

Christians are not without sin, but we repent and ask God to help us to sin no more so we can be a better witness and do our part to bring others to a saving faith in Jesus Christ.

Questions:

1. How often do you test man's laws against Christ's teaching?
2. Does this Scripture mean that only men will deal with lust?
3. How does this verse impact how you respond to those who commit adultery (very external) compared to those who look lustfully?

(Day 68)

> If your right eye causes you to sin, tear it out and throw it away. For it is better that you lose one of your members than that your whole body be thrown into hell. (Matthew 5:29)

Jesus Christ willingly chose to be separated from the Father, for a time, to save us from our sins. Our minds cannot comprehend what a sacrifice this was by Jesus. We have no idea what it would be like since we have never been in that kind of a relationship. Our minds aren't capable of understanding. Anyone that tells you otherwise most likely has a pride issue. God dealt with sin in a radical way: Christ's sacrifice. We must deal with sin radically too. Our Lord does not want us to be mutilating our bodies, but he does want us to realize how much sin costs us and to deal radically with it. Can you imagine the trauma it would cause to see people tearing out their eyes? I say this in jest, but I have heard stories about people truly doing this. Our bodies are a temple of the Lord, and they need to be treated as such for serving our true King. We must see sin how God sees sin and deal with it in a radical way.

Questions:

1. How quick are you to deal with your sin?
2. To what lengths have you gone to not sin? Have you ever had to get out of a relationship to help you stop sinning?
3. How have you counseled others when they come to you, asking for help in dealing with sin? How would you counsel someone if they came to you, asking for help in dealing with sin?

(Day 69)

> And if your right hand causes you to sin, cut it off and throw it away. For if it is better that you lose one of your members than that your whole body go into hell. (Matthew 5:30)

In case Jesus's audience didn't fully understand God's teaching on the truth about sin after the eye example, he went on to another similar example. He took the time to give two separate but very visible examples of how we should deal with sin. Due to the consequences of sin, separation from God, sin must be dealt with in a radical way. Again, mutilation is not what Jesus is promoting here. If that was the case, all of his followers would have been missing limbs or eyes as would current Christians. There is no Scripture telling about his apostles or disciples doing such things. He would have had to be constantly healing his own followers of physical ailments. Jesus wants us to understand just how horrible sin is. Don't ever forget, it took Jesus choosing to sacrifice himself on the cross to pay the debt owed for mankind's sin. Both examples should also give us a little better understanding of just how terrible hell is and the reality that it is for those who aren't covered by the blood of Christ. Sin is not to be trifled with, and the consequences are dire.

Questions:

1. Who or what should we be blaming for our sin? Would it actually make sense to blame our hand?
2. What is the longest you have gone without repenting of a sin, or what sin do you hold onto the most?
3. Has the idea of tearing out your own eye or cutting off your hand changed your opinion of sin? How or why not?

(Day 70)

> It was also said, "Whoever divorces his wife, let him give her a certificate of divorce." But I say to you that everyone who divorces his wife, except on the ground of sexual immorality, makes her commit adultery, and whoever marries a divorced woman commits adultery. (Matthew 5:31–32)

Divorce runs rampant across society today, and so does the carnage it leaves behind. There are also so many different "truths" or ideas about what is right and wrong when it comes to divorce. Thankfully, it is addressed in Scripture. In verses 27 and 28, Jesus made it clear that adultery is a sin, so the bar he has set for us is to not get divorced. The consequences of divorce are so severe and long-lasting that I often wonder if that is why Satan seems so determined to destroy it. The negative impact it has on the adults and the kids is tragic. Don't ever believe it is just the kids who are scarred. I have never found that teaching in the Bible. It is amazing and interesting, although it shouldn't be, how God's truths are proved to be accurate, helpful, and useful in the secular world. Furthermore, it is also sad, discouraging, and disheartening to see how many professing Christians have fallen to the lie that divorce is an acceptable option to a difficult marriage. An older Christian boss I used to know at college once told me, your marriage can be good or it can be bad, but divorce is not an option so you better figure it out. That's not an exact quote, but it gets the point across. I was always confident that he spent time with Christ in prayer and reading the Word. One last thought: If you want a "good" read on divorce, consider *An Unexpected Legacy of Divorce*. You probably haven't heard of it, and there is probably a reason for that.

Questions:

1. How has divorce affected your life, whether through family, friends or personally?
2. When was the last time you heard a sermon on divorce? Do you think such sermons should be avoided?
3. If you are married, have you ever had someone suggest to you that divorce would be a good/okay thing? If you are not married, do you see divorce as an option?

(Day 71)

> "Again you have heard that it was said to those of old, You shall not swear falsely, but shall perform to the Lord what you have sworn." (Matthew 5:33)

Jesus is continuing his direct teaching about specific topics or sins that people have continually struggled with. I think this is one of the more ignored and mocked sins that causes countless problems. The outcome(s) of swearing falsely can also be hard to trace back to the original lie that started the fire. Swearing falsely is lying. James 3:6, And the tongue is a fire, a world of unrighteousness. The tongue is set among our members, staining the whole body, setting on fire the entire course of life, and set on fire by hell. James 3:8, but not human being can tame the tongue. It is a restless evil, full of deadly poison. Taking the time to read all of James 3 would be well worth it when considering the consequences of swearing falsely. With the invention of social media, there seems to be much less accountability for what people say or say/type. What we say does matter and does have consequences. Lies beget lies and hurtful, spiteful communication usually leads to lies (I did not say that, it was not me, so and so told me, etc.).

Questions:

1. How many times have you been hurt by someone swearing falsely?
2. How many times have you seen relationships destroyed based on people swearing falsely?
3. Have you ever had to try and repair your reputation due to someone swearing falsely about you?

(Day 72)

> But I say to you, Do not take an oath at all, either by heaven, for it is the throne of God, or by the earth, for it is the footstool, or by Jerusalem, for it is the city of the great King. (Matthew 5:34–35)

This verse is showing us that in the eyes of the Lord there really is importance to a man keeping his word. Today, a man's word can be a punchline or treated as useless on TV shows. It strikes me that Jesus is taking the time to more clearly define the importance of taking an oath, he is emphasizing the importance of such an act. Jesus goes so far as to tell us to not even take an oath. It seems like he is trying to protect us from backing ourselves into a corner where we might get in a tricky spot of breaking an oath. Our Lord has made it very clear that we are to avoid sinning and a clear way to do that is by not taking an oath. This seems to fit with the flippancy with which we as a society swear by the Lord without giving enough thought to what we are actually saying or doing. We see this in our highest courts while still giving credence to the value of taking an oath, but don't actually put the value to action. Worse yet, this practice has been taught to our kids. It would be appalling listening to just how often and regular a group of kids break oaths no matter where they are (school, church, sports, youth group, etc.). This is definitely an area that we have given ground on even after Jesus explicitly teaches on it.

Questions:

1. When was the last time you gave much thought about giving an oath, making a promise?
2. When was the last time you had a conversation with someone close to you about the importance of keeping your word?
3. How much do you value the character trait of a friend keeping his/her word?

(Day 73)

> And do not take an oath by your head, for you cannot make one hair white or black. (Matthew 5:36)

Moses told us in Numbers 30:2 that if a man vows a vow to the Lord or swears an oath to bind himself by a pledge, he shall not break his word. He shall do according to all that proceeds out of his mouth. Taking an oath, making a pledge, or making a promise has and always will be a big deal to our Lord. We also see here that we cannot even make one hair white or black. We are utterly helpless creatures, completely dependent on the mercy and will of our triune God. Do not take an oath. Jesus has repeated what he already told us in verse 34. Jesus doesn't repeat himself without reason; it is to emphasize an important lesson. Anybody who teaches, whether it is a professor or a coach, repetition is a strategy used to help bring attention to an important lesson. Do not take an oath by heaven, by earth, by Jerusalem, or by your head. What a difference this is to what the world teaches and practices.

Questions:

1. How different do you think the world would be if we could actually trust everyone when they said something?

2. How different would your relationships be if you could completely trust others and/or they could trust you?
3. What would life be like if the world could completely trust Christians?

(Day 74)

> Let what you say be simply "Yes" or "No," anything more than this comes from the devil. (Matthew 5:37)

I love it when God makes it clear what we are to do, say yes, or no. Jesus makes it sound so simple: Say yes or no. That sounds reasonable; our response to people should be simple. It sounds a lot like the acronym KISS—keep it super simple. I have heard that acronym defined differently, but the truth of it remains. We complicate our responses due to peer pressure, trying to appease others, or not knowing the Word well enough and knowing how we should respond. If we continue to spend time in the Word, getting to know the way Jesus has commanded us to live, and then abide by his teachings, we shouldn't get in positions of needing to take oaths. Our decisions should also not be in danger of being swayed if we remain in his truth. Knowing Jesus, knowing the Word (it's the same thing), should lead us to making confident decisions, answering with a yes or no, and then moving ahead to what Jesus has planned for us next. Some decisions may take longer than others. There is nothing wrong with seeking wisdom through Scripture reading and prayer.

Questions:

1. Why can it be so hard for us to simply say yes or no?
2. When is it hard for you to answer honestly?
3. Who can sway you from answering honestly?

(Day 75)

> You have heard that it was said, "An eye for an eye and a tooth for a tooth." But I say to you, Do not resist the one who is evil. But if anyone slaps you on the right cheek, turn to him the other also. (Matthew 5:38–39)

These verses and the ones following are interesting to me due to all the corruption in the world and also to people's belief about dispensationalism. The first time I heard about dispensationalism and turning the cheek happened at Bible college and revolved around Luke 22:36–38 where Jesus told his disciples to take their moneybags if they had one, a knapsack, and to buy a sword. This does seem to be a transition from sending the twelve out two by two with nothing in Luke 10:1ff. Personally, I do believe the Bible teaches us that God works differently in different time periods. This does not mean he is changing his mind, but his plan for the salvation of mankind does look different throughout the ages until he returns. Scripture teaches us to be slow to anger (James 1:19) and that vengeance is the Lord's (Romans 12:19). Romans 12:20–21 goes on to tell us how to deal with our enemies. I do not read in Scripture where Jesus tells us we have to stand by and watch others be beaten. If we can stop violence, then stop it, but do not take vengeance.

Questions:

1. Do you see a difference between stopping violence and taking vengeance?
2. What should we do with a book, like Judges, when thinking about these verses?
3. How do you think you would respond if you were slapped on the cheek?

MATTHEW

(Day 76)

> And if anyone would sue you and take your tunic
> let him have your cloak as well. (Matthew 5:40)

Jesus has now moved us from a physical attack to a monetary loss and/or a loss of comfort. With his teaching on being slow to anger, I don't think we need to do much more here. The loss of a couple of physical items is not the same as being physically beaten. These verses are not saying that these are the only items someone has to keep them warm but that they will lose a tunic and a cloak. If we start adding to what these verses are saying or creating a bunch of hypothetical situations, then we start moving away from what Christ is saying here. If someone wants to sue you for your tunic, let them have it. If they want to sue you for your cloak as well, fine. There is nothing else being used as an example here. Jesus is not teaching about anything else that a person is being sued for.

Questions:

1. What "cloak" or "tunic" would be hard for you to lose and why?
2. What other comparable item would be hard for you to lose and why?
3. Read Matthew 6:19–21. Do you think those verses apply to what Jesus is teaching on here?

(Day 77)

> And if anyone forces you to go one mile, go with
> them two miles. (Matthew 5:41)

Now Jesus is talking about accepting someone, forcing you to walk with them a mile and to then choose to walk with them a second mile. In the context, this would be against your will. I continue to think about Hebrews 13:2: Do not neglect to show hospitality to strangers, for thereby some have entertained angels unaware. Who are we to say, under what circumstance, Christ will use us to bring one of his lost sheep home? You are in the midst of "going" (Matthew 28:19) when you are walking with someone, even if you did not choose to go on that particular walk. We always want to be looking to do our part when it comes to fulfilling the Great Commission, and who knows when God might be planting a seed through us (1 Corinthians 3:4–9)? Jesus Christ is not telling us that we are going on a walk to die; he is simply telling us to go an extra mile. Always be ready to be used, even if it's in a completely unexpected way.

Questions:

1. When was the last time you unexpectedly found yourself in the "go?"
2. When was the last time you thought about doing your role in the Great Commission?
3. Are you ready for the next assignment God has for you?

(Day 78)

> Give to the one who begs from you, and do not refuse the one who would borrow from you.
> (Matthew 5:42)

A few verses ago, Jesus was teaching us to turn the other cheek if someone slaps us, and now he has moved on telling us to give to others. Give to those who beg, and do not refuse the one who would borrow from you. It's interesting that he is having to encourage us to be giving people. I also find it mildly encouraging. Evidently, being generous has always been a bit of a challenge to those who follow Christ. Notice too that he is simply telling us to give, not how much to give or how little to give, but give. There is also no mention of concerning ourselves with what will happen to whatever it is that we give. What Christ has called us to do is to give. When it comes to letting people borrow from you, it's pretty much the same thing. Do not refuse the one who would borrow from you. Simply go ahead and loan them what they are asking for. Sometimes we try to make God's commands more difficult than he intended, or we fret and focus on the unknown instead of obeying what he plainly asks of us.

Questions:

1. Is there a chance that we struggle with obedience due to wanting to be in control?
2. Is there a chance that we want to know the outcome so we can be recognized or get credit?
3. Do you struggle to give? What hinders you from giving more?

(Day 79)

> You have heard that it was said, "You shall love your neighbor and hate your enemy." But I say to you, love your enemies and pray for those who persecute you. (Matthew 5:43–44)

These verses, along with some of David psalms, have been ones that I have wrestled with over the last few years. In Psalm 25:2, David asked God to not let him be put to shame and to not let his enemies exult over him. There are other very direct prayers that he has about his enemies, but I am not going to attempt to discuss those at this point. Another verse I think about when struggling with those who are attacking me is Ephesians 6:12: For we do not wrestle against flesh and blood, but against the rulers, against the authorities, against the cosmic powers over this present darkness, against the spiritual forces of evil in the heavenly places. Remembering who the real enemy is does help me to pray for those who persecute my family and I. I have prayed that Jesus comes to know them as he has mercifully come to know me or that he leads them to repentance. That is the real issue; they are being used or manipulated by Satan. My prayers do not always begin like this, but in time, the Holy Spirit does lead me there.

Questions:

1. Do you find it hard to pray for your enemies? Why or why not?
2. Do you find it hard to pray for those who persecute your kids, family, and friends? Why or why not?
3. When was the last time you prayed for those who persecute you?

(Day 80)

> So that you may be sons of your father who is in heaven. For he makes his sun rise on the just and the unjust. (Matthew 5:45)

Here is the reward for loving our enemies and praying for those who persecute us. This is the desire of us that know Christ as our Lord and Savior, to be sons of our Father who is in heaven. This is part of our obedience, and those who love the Lord obey his commandments (1 John 5:3). This act of loving our enemies and praying for those who persecute you is not what saves us, but that is the outflow of our new heart. For those of us who now know Jesus as the Christ, don't forget that we used to be the unjust, and he made his sun rise on us. Acts 2:47 states that "praising God and having favor with all the people. And the Lord added to their number day by day those who were being saved." Every day, people across the globe are coming to know Jesus as the Christ due to his abundant mercy and grace. Thank you, Lord, for your unending patience with me before I came to worship you and the patience you still have with me (Philippians 1:6).

Questions:

1. Do you ever wish the sun would stop rising on the unjust?
2. How much patience, mercy, and grace did God show you? Remember where you came from.

3. How much mercy, grace, and patience does God still show you? Remember who we are called to be.

(Day 81)

> For if you love those who love you, what reward do you have? Do not even the tax collectors do the same? (Matthew 5:46)

It is easy or at least easier to love those who love you, but there is nothing special, unique, or different about that. An unredeemed person, a pre-Christian even, loves those who love them. How are we showing Christ to others? How are we fulfilling the Great Commission if we aren't doing anything that shows Christ's love? Christ's love those who mocked him, tormented him, tortured him and took him to the cross to savagely kill him. Christ's love is different, and he is who we are called to emulate. He is the bar we are called to live up to. Acts 7:60 states, "And falling to his knees he cried out with a loud voice, 'Lord do not hold this sin against them.' And when he had said this, he fell asleep." Those are Stephen's words just before he dies as he is literally having rocks thrown at him until he dies. That is a different, holy, other love. I can't say I am honestly there yet and can't get there without the redeeming work of Christ.

Questions:

1. How close are you to asking God to forgive people who are bouncing rocks off your head with the intent of killing you?
2. How do you think you would have responded if you were Stephen?
3. God knows are hearts. Should that change the way we share with people?

(Day 82)

> And if you greet only your brothers, what more are you doing than others? Do not even the Gentiles do the same? (Matthew 5:47)

Jesus is now giving an example of trying to succeed at something less than loving others. We are still called to love others, but can we even bring ourselves to greet others? This seems to be a starting point that we shouldn't take lightly. Many of us Christians can't even take the time to acknowledge someone in front of us in a grocery store, as we're walking, or at work. My last sermon I gave was about this, simply being nice and approachable as a Christian. The response afterward was interesting. Some people couldn't handle the fact that this is step one. They struggled with the idea of simply saying hi to someone. I saw this same thing play out in a couple of churches that I actually worked at; one was during Halloween and the other during Christmas. How can we expect to be used by Christ in leading people to him if we can't take seven seconds to say hi? I encourage you to try this; I think you will be surprised. You might be the only person who even takes the time to acknowledge the other person. A simple smile and a hi can go a long way. It takes someone planting the seed for a strong Douglas fir to grow.

Questions:

1. What are your biggest fears when it comes to actually talking to someone face-to-face?
2. How did you come to know Christ? Did someone throw a tract at you, or was it more personal?
3. As a follower of Christ, how does it feel when leaders in church are dismissive of you on a day other than Sunday (it could be on Sunday too)?

(Day 83)

> You therefore must be perfect, as your heavenly
> Father is perfect. (Matthew 5:48)

There it is; that is what is expected of us. If you still live under the law, that is how you will be judged. If you're perfect, you will have earned your way into heaven. If you are not perfect, you will go to hell. Romans 3:10–12 states, "As it is written: None is righteous, no, not one; no one understands; no one seeks for God. All have turned aside; together they have become worthless; no one does good, not even one." That is the truth, whether you want to believe it or not or how many people tell you you're a good person. God's word is truth. You will not reach perfection on your own, and therefore you deserve an eternity in hell. Thankfully, there is an alternative! Put your faith in Jesus Christ! Please! Accept the fact that you are not perfect (a sinner), like the rest of mankind, and that you need Jesus Christ as your Savior, and he will happily stand in your place before the Father. It is okay if it doesn't make sense. It won't. That's why it is called faith (Hebrews 11:1). You are already a faithful person. Your faith is just in yourself, believing that you are perfect. Instead, put your faith in Jesus Christ.

Questions:

1. Have you ever met someone who has amazing faith in themselves? What was that conversation like? How did it make you feel? If you haven't, I'd encourage you to meet more people. We all need to "go."
2. Does the idea of being perfect scare you? Is perfection something we should take flippantly?
3. How do you feel knowing that you can't be perfect? Is there any chance that brings you peace?

(Day 84)

> Beware of practicing your righteousness before other people in order to be seen by them, for then you will have no reward from your Father who is in heaven. (Matthew 6:1)

We always want to be pointing the world to God the Father. The work that Jesus Christ did was to allow us to have a relationship with the Father. Christ's work gives us forgiveness of sin, which allows us to commune directly to the Father. We don't need and shouldn't want to be seen. We want people to see Christ's work and come to know the loving and just Father. Christians are mouthpieces; we are called to use our God-given gifts to help fulfill the Great Commission. Second Corinthians 5:20 states, "Therefore, we are ambassadors for Christ, God making his appeal through us. We implore you on behalf of Christ, be reconciled to God." That is who we are to be. That is who I want to be. I ask the Holy Spirit on a regular basis to help me be a good, honest, and true ambassador. Help me to speak God's truth boldly for the glory of God (Ephesians 6:19). This is something to put at the forefront when you are looking for a church. Who is your pastor pointing to? Who do you want to be giving you rewards?

Questions:

1. What are your priorities when you look for a pastor?
2. When was the last time you spoke the Word boldly?
3. How important is recognition to you?

(Day 85)

> Thus, when you give to the needy, sound no trumpet before you, as the hypocrites do in the synagogues and in the streets, that they may be

> praised by others. Truly, I say to you, they have
> received their reward. (Matthew 6:2)

As you read Scripture, as you read the truth, it will become very clear to you that Christians are not to be boastful people. That does not mean we have to be boring people, lacking zeal and joy, by no means. When we are going about the Lord's work, seek praise from him. Be quiet and do your work with joy. When you give to the needy, give joyfully and then go about your business. Who do you want to receive your reward from? This needs to be modeled to our kids and other youth as we live in a time of great trumpet blowers for doing nothing at all. We are in a very "look at me" time in history, and it has infiltrated the church (hypocrites in the synagogue). Jesus was a very intense person. If you don't believe that, I encourage you to reread or read Scripture. We can be people of fervor, just point others to our God. I wanted to quote a verse from later in this chapter, but we will get there soon enough. Passionately serve the Lord, and keep the focus on him.

Questions:

1. Do you live a passionate life? How or why not?
2. Is it hard for you to give (time, money, food, etc.) without being recognized?
3. Is there a chance we need to be careful who we emulate (hypocrites in the synagogues)? How do we protect ourselves from emulating the wrong person?

(Day 86)

> But when you give to the needy, do not let your
> left hand no what your right hand is doing,
> (Matthew 6:3)

It should be clear by now, but when Jesus is repeating things or teaching the same lesson with multiple examples, we should be paying close attention. He is not unprepared, like a normal human teacher, or running out of things to say to kill time; it is for emphasis. If you take a moment and think about it, not letting one hand know what the other hand is doing is tricky. Jesus is telling us, it may be tricky for a variety of reasons to not let others know when you are giving to the needy, but you definitely shouldn't be making a show of it. If you get "caught," don't panic; that is not the point. God is not in heaven, saying, "Nice try, but Billy Bob saw you give to the needy." Where is your heart at? Are you seeking praise from people? Let your giving be between you and the Lord. I'm confident saying, it would be good if your spouse knows, if you're married, and probably even encourage you are one. Also, please notice, he did not say giving money. Giving can look different due to your resources.

Questions:

1. How are you doing at giving? What can you give when you see a need?
2. It appears to be a given that you are giving? What do you think about that?
3. This is not to make us feel bad or to start ranking who the best givers are, but consider how you could improve when it comes to giving to the needy.

(Day 87)

> So that your giving may be in secret. And your Father who sees in secret will reward you. (Matthew 6:4)

This is a continuation of verse 3, but there is plenty to think of. Plain and simple: Thank you, Jesus, your giving should be in secret. He has given us examples of how to give. And then just in case we still don't understand, he states it plainly. Don't practice your righteousness in front of others. Keep your trumpets in their cases. Do the best you can to not be showing off, and let your giving be done in secret. We are also told again that this will lead to a reward from the best reward giver. Jesus doesn't say you might be rewarded but that your Father who sees in secret will reward you. He does not say what the reward will be, or even if we will be getting it on this side of heaven, but he will reward us. It's hard for me to not want, wish, and hope for a physical, tangible reward right now that I can touch, see, and feel, but an eternal reward is forever. Jesus does not specify one way or the other, but we shouldn't fret over the gift (Luke 11:11–13).

Questions:

1. Is it hard for you to even consider the idea of giving a gift in secret?
2. This is and evidently has always been a struggle. Why is that?
3. What reward would you want?

(Day 88)

> And when you pray you must not be like the hypocrites. For they love to stand and pray in the synagogues and at the street corners, that they may be seen by others. Truly, I say to you, they have received their reward. (Matthew 6:5)

Jesus is giving some of the same advice here. The context is a little different. He is now specifically talking about prayer, which could still have to do with helping people in need. Hopefully, some of your prayer time is focused on praise and thanksgiving too. Do not try to be a showboat when you are praying. The example Christ is presenting to us here is of people trying to draw attention to themselves. If you ever find yourself around a spiritual leader that is attempting to draw attention to themselves, be suspicious. If you spend time with other believers that constantly point to their "greatness," be wary. Mature Christians are always thanking Christ for his work on the cross, looking to the Holy Spirit for guidance and wisdom, or praising the Father. True followers of Christ deflect glory and/or attention because they know who they are apart from God working in and through them. It is hard to overlook that Jesus again specifically mentions this issue inside the synagogue. Make spending time in the Word and praying a priority so you don't fall prey to false teaching.

Questions:

1. How do you protect yourself from falling into hypocrisy?
2. It is implied here that we are praying. How has your prayer been today?
3. How do people know if you spend lots of time in prayer? Should it matter if people know how much time you spend in prayer?

(Day 89)

> But when you pray, go into your room and shut the door and pray to your Father who is in secret. And your Father who sees in secret will reward you. (Matthew 6:6)

Jesus said that when we pray, not if we want to pray, it should be a given that Christians are praying. If you haven't prayed yet today, please consider going and doing so right now. Prayer needs to become a priority in every Christian's life, think about committing to prioritizing it into your daily schedule. Pray to your Father; we have that direct link to him due to Christ's work on the cross. the curtain has been torn. Our Father wants that time with us—doesn't need but wants. Some people are unaware that we have this privilege of talking directly to our Father whenever we want. We can't ignore the continued emphasis from Jesus about being rewarded. It has been a focus in the first six verses of chapter 6. It is okay to seek rewards from our heavenly Father; they are everlasting. Where and how are we to pray privately. If your room happens to be busy, find a quiet, private space. If your whole house is busy, take a drive, shut off the radio, and pray to him privately. Don't be a can't doer when it comes to prayer. Make it happen often and frequently. Remember, it isn't supposed to be a show.

Questions:

1. Can people or a group of people really stop you from praying?
2. What if you only have a moment to spare, would it count to pray then? What if you can only pray quietly in your head, would that count.
3. At this point, what are we specifically or directly *not* supposed to be doing when it comes to prayer?

(Day 90)

> And when you pray, do not heap up empty phrases as the Gentiles do, for they think that they will be heard for their many words. (Matthew 6:7)

Jesus is again making it clear that Christians should be praying; it's not an option. Empty phrases aren't what God is looking for. Scripture teaches us he is looking for a genuine heart from those who worship him. Hebrews 10:22 states, "Let us draw near with a true heart in full assurance of faith, with our hearts sprinkled clean from an evil conscience and our bodies washed with pure water." He will see through our fluff and games when we are praying. God cannot be tricked. Psalm 139:2 states, "You know when I sit down and when I rise up, you discern my thoughts from afar." Empty words, or the "right" Christian's words, are not what he wants. Your heavenly Father wants a genuine, authentic, and trusting personal relationship with you. You can trick your friends and family with your spiritual talk, not that that helps you build a better relationship with them, but your Father truly knows you. Don't ever forget who the God you worship is—omnipotent, omniscience, omnipresence, and sovereign.

Questions:

1. Are you comfortable bringing your concerns, fear, and doubts to God? Why or why not?
2. What do you think holds people back from being honest with God?
3. Where are you at when it comes to being genuine and authentic with your heavenly Father when you pray (ex: 1—not so good, 10—you are completely genuine and authentic)?

(Day 91)

> Do not be like them, for your Father knows what you need before you ask him. (Matthew 6:8)

We are not to be like them. Followers of Jesus Christ, do not be like them. Do not be like the hypocrites when it comes to praying. There isn't ever a good time to be a hypocrite, but Jesus is giving us a special lesson on not being hypocritical when it comes to prayer. We also always need to remember who we are supposed to be pointing to, who we should direct others to. If we want glory from our heavenly Father, if we want to be rewarded from God, then we need to always be pointing others to him. If we truly love others, then our desire should be for the pre-Christian to see God the Father, not us. We are nothing but a mouthpiece, a servant, an ambassador for God. If you want glory from man, then go ahead and make yourself the center of attention. Jesus can't be clearer here: Do not be like them. John 3:30 states, "He must increase, but I must decrease." Those are the words of John the Baptist. He is definitely a role model.

Questions:

1. What do you think about Jesus telling us not to be like them? Isn't that kind of being exclusive?

2. How should our prayer life be affected when we read that Jesus tells us that our Father knows what we need before we ask?
3. How did you do last week when it came to being an ambassador for our triune God?

(Day 92)

> Pray then like this: "Our Father in heaven, hallowed be your name. (Matthew 6:9)

Good teachers are taught to give solutions, not just tell others what not to do. Knowing what not to do is good, but knowing what to do instead makes things easier. Everyone is going to be doing something. As a Christian, we are not to disengage but to engage. Jesus is now going to teach us how to pray. How often do you think of the only true God as your Father? How often do you approach him as a perfect Father? That is how he describes himself, how he wants to be seen, and how he wants to be approached by those of us who have been covered by Christ's blood. It might be worth your time to look into what the Bible teaches us about the attributes of a father, not what the world teaches but what the Bible teaches. He deserves, commands, and demands to be treated as holy. Is this different from what the world teaches us, different from what pre-Christians believe about our heavenly Father? Where do you get your truth from? Is there more than one truth giver? John 18:38 states, "Pilate said to him, 'What is truth?'" If this is where you are at, bring it to God.

Questions:

1. Is it easy or hard for you to approach God as your Father? Why?
2. When was the last time your called him Father or referred to as Father when you were speaking to him?
3. What does it look like to treat our Father as holy?

(Day 93)

> Your kingdom come, your will be done, on earth as it is in heaven. (Matthew 6:10)

Do you see the contrast that is being presented here? His kingdom come; his will be done—be done on earth as it is done in heaven. God's ways are holy, different, other. Do you desire that his kingdom come, or are you in love with the world and the way things are? First John 2:15 states, "Do not love the world or the things in the world. If anyone loves the world, the love of the Father is not in him." We are also called to be joyful and content. But do you desire and crave for his kingdom to come? Are you excited for his kingdom to come? Are you ready for his kingdom to come? His kingdom is drastically different from what we have here on earth. His will be done, and never doubt that his will will be done. Do you want his will to be done? Do you ask for his will to be done? Hopefully, the truth that the one and only sovereign God's will will be done, brings you peace and comfort. In all honesty, that truth is what keeps me sane. To worship a god whose will could be thwarted would be terrifying and unimaginably frightening.

Questions:

1. When was the last time you asked that God's will be done in your life? How do you think you'd respond if his will was different than what you wanted?
2. When was the last time you prayed for his kingdom to come (Revelation 22:20)?
3. What do you think about the truth we read about in the Bible about the dichotomy we see about earth and heaven?

(Day 94)

> Give us this day our daily bread. (Matthew 6:11)

Unfortunately, I do not remember what book I was reading or who I was talking to about this verse, but he pointed out that this verse specifically mentions our daily bread. Jesus did not say to pray to give us a full pantry, freezer, refrigerator, or cupboard(s). That is not to say that something is wrong if those things are full in your house. Jesus also didn't direct us to pray for the best food, whatever that is to you, but to simply pray to be given our daily bread. Maybe this has to do with being content. Philippians 4:11 states, "Not that I am speaking of being in need, for I have learned in whatever situation I am to be content." Paul is another example of a great role model. I think reading about how the Israelites responded to the manna and quail could also give us some guidance here. It did not take them long to start complaining about both the manna and the quail. When I start complaining and whining about my lot in life, I start to think about how many people today do not have their daily bread or even clean water. Thank you, Lord, for giving me my daily bread.

Questions:

1. When was the last time you had to go without your daily bread?
2. How do you think your faith would be impacted or hold up if you didn't have daily bread?
3. When was the last time you recognized your dependence on God for daily bread? Do you believe you are dependent on God for daily bread?

(Day 95)

> And forgive us our debts, as we have also forgiven our debtors. (Matthew 6:12)

Forgiveness and Christianity go hand in hand, and our Savior Jesus Christ, the role model of role models, who we strive to be like, is forgiveness. In verses 14 and 15, he again highlighted the importance of forgiveness. Here we read in the Lord's Prayer that we are to ask for forgiveness of our debts (sins). Once we ask for that forgiveness, we also need to accept that forgiveness, believe in Christ's sacrifice, which enables us to be forgiven and allows us to come to the Father. Struggling with truly believing and living as forgiven sinners is a struggle for Christians. Not believing in the total and complete power of Christ's work on the cross to forgive us of our past sins, current sins, and future sins is a weapon and a lie from Satan himself. Satan is the father of lies. When he speaks his native tongue, he is lying (John 8:44), and he hinders many Christians by lying to them about the power of Jesus Christ's sacrifice. We also read here that we are to forgive our debtors, those who have sinned against us. We will look at our forgiving others more closely in verses 14 and 15.

Questions:

1. What sins are you struggling with accepting that you have been forgiven of? Why?
2. What sins are easiest for you to accept forgiveness of? Why?
3. How do you live as a forgiven follower of Jesus Christ? Have you ever met a Christian that doesn't seem as if they believe they are forgiven?

(Day 96)

> And lead us not into temptation, but deliver us from evil. (Matthew 6:13)

This is another example of where the Christian needs to show humility. We need to ask to not be led into temptation and to be delivered from evil. Our flesh is corrupt. We are fallen people. And if we don't ask for help in battling our fallen nature, then we will lose the daily battles. We need help when it comes to dealing with temptation. First Corinthians 10:13 states, "No temptation has overtaken you that is not common to man. God is faithful, and he will not let you be tempted beyond your ability, but with the temptation he will also provide a way of escape, that you may be able to endure." Remember, Jesus was tempted (Matthew 4:1–11), so we will be tempted, but it is for our growth in becoming more like Christ. Ask to not be led into temptation, but walk in faith that our Lord will be there to help us face the temptation and grow through it. We aren't told to put on the whole armor of God without reason (Ephesians 6:10–20). Never forget that the war has been won, but we are in a battle.

Questions:

1. Do you struggle believing that you need help to defeat temptation? Why or why not?
2. Have you ever struggled with believing that God won't tempt you beyond your ability? Why or why not?
3. When was the last time you prayed for help before you went out into the battlefield?

(Day 97)

> For if you forgive others their trespasses, your heavenly Father will also forgive you, but if you do not forgive others their trespasses, neither will your Father forgive your trespasses. (Matthew 6:14–15)

Jesus has made it clear that we need to forgive others when they sin against us. In these two verses, he stated it clearly that if we don't forgive others, then our Father will not forgive you your trespasses. I have heard this verse taken to the point that people will try to say that someone is not saved if you don't forgive others, or you could lose your salvation if you don't forgive. I have also seen it used as a weapon by the offending party. Our salvation is not based on works but by grace. Romans 11:6 states, "But if it is by grace, it is no longer on the basis of works; otherwise grace would no longer be grace." We are called to forgive. It is a commandment, not a suggestion but a commandment. In verse 12, it seems like it is a given that we will forgive others. Remember, there is a difference between forgiveness and reconciliation. Luke 7:47 states, "Therefore I tell you, her sins, which are many, are forgiven—for she loved much. But he who is forgiven little loves little." Don't ever forget how much you have been forgiven, and it should make it easier to forgive.

Question:

1. Do you think you have been forgiven much or little? What leads you to your belief?
2. How often do you find yourself slipping into the belief that you are saved by works?
3. Do you find it is more difficult to forgive someone or to be reconciled? Why?

(Day 98)

> And when you fast, do not look gloomy like the hypocrites, for they disfigure their faces that their fasting may be seen by others. Truly, I say to you, they have received their reward. (Matthew 6:16)

We see Jesus using a lot of the same language here that he used when he was teaching about prayer. We are also dealing with the same heart issue and the issue of hypocrisy. Do you seek rewards and attention from men while putting the emphasis on yourself, or do you want to be rewarded by the Father and continue to help point others to him? Fasting is a spiritual discipline, like prayer, that should be a normal practice Christians, but it is not meant to be used as an attention getting device. It also reads like Jesus is assuming that his followers are fasting when you fast. Don't turn fasting into something it's not, with a bunch or rules and regulations with how often and for how long. Fasting is a personal thing between you and your heavenly Father. Don't ever get sucked into a fasting competition or something to brag about; that would be seeking an award from man.

Questions:

1. If you aren't fasting, why is that?
2. When was the last time you had a conversation or heard a sermon about fasting?
3. Why do you think hypocrisy was and is still such an issue? Is it only a church issue, or does it exist by those outside the church too?

(Day 99)

> But when you fast, anoint your head and wash your face. (Matthew 6:17)

He is telling us exactly what to do when you fast—when, not if. We are supposed to do just the opposite of what the hypocrites do, not just for the purpose of being different or unique but because our Father is telling us to be different. The only time I have put oil on my head is to combat dry skin. In this verse, it has something to do with looking healthy, such as being well fed. People who are well fed and healthy don't look gloomy. He also tells us to wash our face. This sounds a lot like putting on your best clothes, looking your best and acting your best. Do not give any inkling that you are fasting, sick in any way, or not feeling your best. Zechariah 7:5 states, "Say to all the people of the land and the priests, 'When you fasted and mourned in the fifth month and in the seventh, for these seventy years, was it for me that you fasted?'" When you fast, just as Jesus fasted, who is it for?

Questions:

1. What would you think about committing to fasting? Do you think it is something you could/should do? Why or why not?
2. What does the world teach about fasting? To the pre-Christian, what has fasting become?

3. Would it be strange for Satan to attack something that our Father teaches us to do?

(Day 100)

> That your fasting may not be seen by others but by your Father who is in secret. And your Father who sees in secret will reward you. (Matthew 6:18)

Our fasting is not to be seen by others, period. This can be tricky if you are married or acting weird around your kids during mealtime. Keep the heart of why you are fasting as your focus; it is a spiritual discipline between you and your heavenly Father. Joel 2:12 states, "'Yet even now,' declares the Lord, 'return to me with all your heart, with fasting, with weeping, and with mourning.'" Sometimes I will try to give my wife a heads-up or a hint because I do want to be rewarded by my father. Furthermore, I want to be fasting correctly as my Father has directed me to. Isaiah 58:3 states, "'Why have we fasted, and you see it not? Why have we humbled ourselves, and you take no knowledge of it?' Behold, in the day of your fast you seek your own pleasure, and oppress all your workers." Fasting is something we should be doing as Christians, but make sure it is a godly fast and not a worldly fast.

Questions:

1. Are you excited about possibly refocusing on fasting? Why or why not?
2. What do you think the biggest hindrance is to Christians fasting on a regular basis?
3. Will you be content with however God decides to reward you? Do you trust in the perfection of his gift giving?

(Day 101)

> Do not lay up for yourselves treasures on earth, where moth and rust destroy and where thieves break in and steal. (Matthew 6:19)

Earth is fleeting. It has an expiration date, and so does every human. When earth will come to an end has already been decided by the triune God, it is not up to mankind to decide when or how earth will come to an end. Mankind can't prolong earth's existence or end it early. Since these things are true, doesn't it make sense to ease up on how much treasure we are storing up here on earth? Jesus gives us a very practical reason to not lay up treasures for ourselves on earth. Moths and rust literally destroy things, and thieves are real. It seems that everyone is looking for a good return on their work or an excellent investment opportunity, which is reasonable. Everything on earth will come to an end, including us. So investing in earthly possessions aren't all they are cracked up to be. Look for a better investment, something that will last for eternity. I wonder what that investment would be?

Questions:

1. How do you do with laying up treasures on earth?
2. If money is a resource given to us by God or entrusted to us by God, how should we go about using or handling it?
3. Thinking about things coming to an end on earth or not lasting, what do you think about leaving a legacy? What kind of legacy do you want to leave? Is there a legacy that moths and rust can't destroy or thieves can't steal?

(Day 102)

> But lay up for yourselves treasures in heaven, where neither moth nor rust destroys and where thieves do not break in and steal. (Matthew 6:20)

Jesus has again kindly told us where to lay up our treasures. We are told to lay up or store up treasures in heaven. Nothing that is being stored up in heaven—our salvation for instance—can be destroyed by moth or rust, nor can thieves break in and steal. That sounds like a great place to store up treasure. What kind of treasures can we hope to lay up in heaven? What about treasures from our Father? I imagine those are eternally secure. That makes me think, what kind of gifts do I want from the Father—earthly gifts or heavenly gifts—that I can't even comprehend right now? Giving and taking care of those in need to the best of our abilities seems to be valued by God (Matthew 25:33–40; James 2:16–17; Luke 10:25–37; 1 Timothy 4:8). The Bible does seem to teach that it is okay to seek these things, just don't be boastful or showy about it, then your gift would come from man where it can be destroyed or stolen.

Questions:

1. How often do you strive to seek gifts from our Father? Why?
2. How often do you strive to seek gifts from humans? Why?
3. Do you ever think of salvation as a gift? If it is from our heavenly Father, how can it be destroyed or stolen? Who has that kind of power?

(Day 103)

> For where your treasure is, there your heart is also. (Matthew 6:21)

So does what we treasure lead our heart, or does our heart lead are treasure? If we get our heart right, then the treasure we desire will change. Hopefully, we are all seeing that our Father is interested in our heart. We have seen this when it comes to prayer, fasting, and now with what we treasure. In every person's heart, there are people that they treasure—friends, family, spouse, etc.—and they are also our treasure. What we treasure, we spend time with improving, nurturing, and refining. This could even just be with our hobbies. Ideally, God has a big piece of your heart, and you then treasure time with him to get to know him better. The better we know someone, the better we know how to please them or make them happy. It is the same with knowing our Savior. If you want to know how much you treasure the heavenly Father, and if he is in your heart, ask yourself and answer honestly, how much time do you spend cultivating your relationship with him?

Questions:

1. Where does the triune God rank in your gaggle of treasures?
2. How do you show what it is that you treasure most?
3. Who or what owns the majority of your heart?

(Day 104)

> The eye is the lamp of the body. So, if your eye
> is healthy, your whole body will be full of light.
> (Matthew 6:22)

To be clear, you want to be known as a person full of light. You will see in the next verse that the other option is darkness. Your eyes feed your body, feed what you see, what you focus on, and what you fill yourself with. If you continually look to things that Jesus Christ values, then you will be filling yourself with light. Filling yourself with light also has to do with who you surround yourself with, who you literally look to, who you want to model yourself after. First Corinthians 15:33 states, "Do not be deceived: 'Bad company ruins good morals.'" Other translations of that verse say, bad company corrupts. If you are deceived, it is because you are deceiving yourself. We all know who we are around impacts our behavior. Proverbs 27:17 states, "Iron sharpens iron, and one man sharpens another." Who do you fill your eyes with?

Questions:

1. How much do you desire to be healthy?
2. How closely do you pay attention to your diet and getting exercise?
3. Is your company making you feel brighter?

(Day 105)

> But if your eye is bad, your whole body will be full of darkness. If then the light in you is darkness, how great is that darkness? (Matthew 6:23)

Dealing with down or depressing seasons doesn't mean your whole body is darkness. We are under constant attack; spiritual warfare is a real thing. This truth is not to lead us to living in terror or to be fearful, but we must always be alert and aware of what is really going on. First John 4:4 states, "Little children, you are far from God and have overcome them, for he who is in you is greater than he who is in the world." That being said, do not let yourself succumb or be filled with darkness. Furthermore, if you are full of darkness, there is still hope. Repent, look to Jesus Christ who is the source of light, admit that you're a sinner, ask for forgiveness, and ask Jesus into your life. Revelation 3:30 states, "Behold, I stand at the door and knock. If anyone hears my voice and opens the door, I will come in to him and eat with him, and he with me." Don't worry, when Jesus calls, you will hear him; just don't be slow in answering.

Questions:

1. How are you when it comes to overcoming the times spent in the desert?
2. When you walk through the valley of death, how do you keep walking (Psalm 23:4)?
3. Are you good at recognizing when you're filling yourself with darkness? How long does it take you to avert your

eyes, to get out of that situation, or lessen the time around those people?

(Day 106)

> No one can serve two masters, for either he will hate the one and love the other, or he will be devoted to the one and despise the other. You cannot serve God and money. (Matthew 6:24)

This verse is pretty straightforward and isn't tricky to understand at face value. The idea of serving two masters is an idea from the enemy. It is a fallacy, and those who fall for it will feel the effects. Life is full of slippery slopes and numerous different temptations from the author of lies. Revelation 3:16 states, "So, because you are lukewarm, and neither hot nor cold, I will spit you out of my mouth." We cannot afford to do anything less than desperately cling to our Lord and Savior. The devil is real, and he hates us. He knows he has lost our souls, so he wants to try and make us ineffective. Exodus 34:14 states, "For you shall worship no other god, for the Lord, whose name is Jealous, is a Jealous God." It is hard not to notice that money is specifically mentioned. The rich young ruler is a great parable to take a look at before moving on (Mark 10:17–22).

Questions:

1. What/who does rival your affection? What master tempts to draw you away from the triune God?
2. When you are in a valley or in the desert, what/who do you run to?
3. Do you believe that the devil hates you, wants you to feel useless, and not use your spiritual gifts to bring glory to God? He will also try to distract you with fool's gold.

(Day 107)

> Therefore I tell you, do not be anxious about your life, what you will eat or what you will drink, not about your body, what you will put on. Isn't life more than food, and the body more than clothing? (Matthew 6:25)

The battle with anxiety is a real thing, and I have always found it interesting that Jesus directly teaches about it in numerous verses. The Bible teaches us that anxiety is an attack from the true enemy, Satan himself. The best way to combat such attacks is to go to prayer, Scripture, or sing songs of praise. Jesus isn't speaking figuratively here. Do not be anxious. Anxiety and fear are closely related, and it is definitely a tool that is used in the world. Personally, I relate to struggling with my faith. God is sovereign; nothing is going to surprise him or happen without him ordaining it, and that should bring me peace. It is an area that I focus on in my prayer time, and I can say that I have gotten better at dealing with fear, anxiety, and faith, and that is definitely thanks to the Holy Spirit. Living without being controlled by anxiety is putting my faith in action. It's another area I will be working on until I arrive in heaven.

Questions:

1. How would you describe yourself when it comes to anxiousness?
2. Do you think other people would describe you as an anxious person? Have you ever had a discussion about anxiety?
3. Do you agree that faith and anxiety are related? Why or why not?

(Day 108)

> Look at the birds of the air: they neither sow nor reap not gather into barns, and yet your heavenly

> Father feeds them. Are you not of more value than they? (Matthew 6:26)

Please give notice to Jesus talking about food in verse 25 and now again in verse 26. What does the Lord's Prayer say about food? Give us your daily bread. Food is a real need and a real humanitarian crisis in some areas and not to be taken lightly. The need is even present in some areas right here in America. It is also an area where people get separated into classes, and haughtiness can be a problem. Thankfully, my taste palate is as advanced as a good steak, and they are much cheaper to cook at my house. Please come to realize, if you don't already, Christ's question is rhetorical. We are made in God's image; birds are not. If our Lord is taking care of the birds that are not made in his image, then he will take care of us. For me, the real rub can come down to how much I like or trust (faith), how he is taking care of my wife, kids, and I while I am supposed to be leading. Do I have faith that the things my wife, kids, and I go through could be helping to form us into the people we were created to be and that everything is just how our triune God has planned it?

Questions:

1. What does the world teach us when it comes to comparing humans to animals?
2. When was the last time you contemplated how much value you have in your heavenly Father's eyes?
3. Do you see yourself the same way your heavenly Father sees you?

(Day 109)

> And which of you by being anxious can add a single hour to his span of life? (Matthew 6:27)

Anxiousness does nothing good for us, either mentally or physically. Absolutely nothing positive comes from being filled or controlled by anxiety. There is an element of pride sneaking in when it comes to being anxious, thinking that we know better than our Savior. If the God of the universe would just listen to me and do things my way, then things would be better. Your theology of God, which is known as theology proper, is of utmost importance, and do not let anyone ever tell you differently. Make sure you are letting the Bible teach you who your heavenly Father is, not humanity. He has revealed himself to us through his Word. Don't add to it or take away from it. Always remember who you are, a completely fallen being saved by the blood of Christ and who the triune God is, the one true holy God and Creator of the entire universe. We can't even add one hour to our lives, but he does not need our advice when he describes who he is.

Questions:

1. How do you feel knowing you can't even add one hour to your life? Do you believe that is true?
2. How well do you think your heavenly Father knows you? Do you believe that he created you and that you are his?
3. What is your first response when you start to feel anxious?

(Day 110)

> And why are you anxious about clothing? Consider the lilies of the field, how they grow: they neither toil nor spin. (Matthew 6:28)

Now Jesus is hitting on clothing, which he also mentioned in verse 25. The text almost makes it sound like he is astonished or that we should be ashamed about being anxious when it comes to clothing. A lot of this attack comes from the world yet again. Yes, you have a shirt, but it's not the right shirt. Yes, you have a sweatshirt, but it's not the right brand. On and on, it goes with every piece of clothing from our head to our feet. Remember Matthew 3:6: Now John wore a garment of camel's hair and a leather belt around his waist, and his food was locusts and wild honey. Food and clothing are both mentioned there, and they are both in a very simple form. Our kids are ruthlessly attacked when it comes to clothing, which leads to anxiety. Women are a close second (fashion). We need to show and live a better way. Why are you anxious about clothing? Don't be—easier said than done. Welcome to Christianity.

Questions:

1. How much time and money do you spend on clothing?
2. How much attention and concern does Jesus give to the "right" clothing?
3. How can you do better for your kids and family when it comes to clothing? What does the Bible say compared to what the world is telling us?

(Day 111)

> Yet I tell you, even Solomon in all his glory was
> not arrayed like one of these. (Matthew 6:29)

Solomon was a man of wealth, which is a huge understatement. He could have and did have the finest of everything, including food and clothing. Even with all his money and the finest fashion designers, he still didn't look as good as the lilies of the field. After all his toiling and spinning and arguably wasted resources on clothing, he still couldn't top wild plants. If the triune God is going to care for plants in such a magnificent way, shouldn't we trust him when it comes to him caring for us? We should also take care with where we put our time and resources. God has given us gifts to use for his glory, and we are called to be good stewards of those gifts. If we are going to struggle with anxiety, it shouldn't be about clothing, unless you don't actually have any clothing, or you don't have clothing to keep yourself warm.

Questions:

1. Can you relate to toiling over something and not having the outcome you hoped for?
2. How are you doing when it comes to being a good steward of what your heavenly Father has given you and entrusted to you?
3. What is a fun or funny story about something you toiled over and then regretted later?

(Day 112)

> But if God so clothes the grass of the field, which today is alive and tomorrow is thrown into the oven, will he not much more clothe you, O you of little faith? (Matthew 6:30)

As a follower of Jesus Christ, I do not want to be known as having little faith. I want to be known as one of the men that can be read about in Hebrews 11. Hebrews 11:1 states, "Now faith is the assurance of things hoped for, the conviction of things not seen." That is the biblical definition of faith; any other definition falls short. If God is clothing the grass of the field in such a magnificent way, then we should be trusting that he will clothe us. Our faith starts to waver when we are not content or satisfied with how he is clothing us. There is a chance that too many Christians look to the wrong role model when we think about what we supposedly need when it comes to clothes. No matter how great someone thinks their faith is, there is always room to grow. We all need to stay humble and continually ask our heavenly Father to make our faith greater so that we are always growing in our ability to serve him.

Questions:

1. What does shake or challenge your faith?

2. What are you currently focusing on when it comes to your spiritual growth?
3. Are you ever challenged by thinking that you have arrived when it comes to a spiritual discipline?

(Day 113)

> Therefore do not be anxious, saying, "What shall we eat?" or "What shall we drink?" or "What shall we wear?" (Matthew 6:31)

Here we are, back to verse 25. Do not be anxious. Jesus has continued to specifically reference food and clothing while talking about fighting off anxiety. He has added drink in this verse, which is obviously closely related to food; it's a critical sustenance. These are all such basic needs that it makes me think just how dire things must have been for the apostles and disciples as they traveled with Christ. Luke 9:58 states, "And Jesus said to them, 'Foxes have holes, and birds of the air have nests, but the Son of Man has nowhere to lay his head.'" I can't truly relate to having anxiety over these things. Unfortunately, my anxiety, when it comes to food, drink, and clothing, is very superficial. Did I get the right sauce with my steak? Do I have to drink the clean, clear, and sanitized tap water again? I wish I could have gotten the blue shirt instead of the black one. Lord willing, I will never know what true anxiety looks like when it comes to food, drink, and clothing.

Questions:

1. Do you treat anxiety as a sin as being disobedient to our heavenly Father?
2. Have you ever thought that the time of Christ's earthly ministry was peaceful and easy?
3. When was the last time you thanked and/or praised God for the simple things in your life?

(Day 114)

> For the Gentiles seek after all these things, and your heavenly Father knows that you need them all. (Matthew 6:32)

The implication is that we should be better than the gentiles when it comes to having faith in our triune God. The Christian's faith should be stronger than gentiles. We are worshipping the one true God, and who knows what variety of gods individual gentiles are worshipping? The options seem to be never ending. These past few verses have been pointing to faith and then contentment with how our Lord is meeting our needs. Proverbs 30:8–9 states, "Remove far from me falsehood and lying; give me neither poverty nor riches; feed me with the food that is needful for me, lest I be full and deny you and say, 'Who is the Lord?' Or lest I be poor and steal and profane the name of my God." Nowhere in the Bible does it say that following Christ will be easy. Jesus tells us, his yoke is easy, but do we like his yoke, or do we think the yoke of the world is better and easier?

Questions:

1. What in the world tempts you the most when it comes to pulling your attention away from Jesus Christ?
2. Have you ever prayed for neither poverty nor riches?
3. Have you ever considered the dangers of being rich?

(Day 115)

> But seek first the kingdom of God and his righteousness, and all these things will be added to you. (Matthew 6:33)

I always appreciate being told the solution, no matter the venue or topic. Christians need to keep the kingdom of God as their number one. First and foremost, those who call Jesus the Christ and recognize him as their Savior should be seeking the kingdom of God and his righteousness. Nothing else the world offers can even come close to comparing to the lasting worth of seeking the kingdom of God and his righteousness. Just like the hymn says, my hope is built on nothing less, and all other ground is sinking sand. Luke 6:47–48a states, "Everyone who comes to me and hears my words and does them, I will show you what he is like: he is like a man building a house, who dug deep and laid the foundation on the rock." The Christian is not called to just be a hearer but a doer of God's word. If you are not a doer, I pray that you are moving in that direction. If you believe that you are a doer, do not become complacent.

Questions:

1. Where are you when it comes to seeking the kingdom of God and his righteousness?
2. How are you doing when it comes to being a hearer of the truth that is found in the Bible?
3. How are you at being a doer when it comes to doing what the Holy Spirit has called you to do?

(Day 116)

> Therefore do not be anxious about tomorrow, for tomorrow will be anxious for itself. Sufficient for the day is its own trouble. (Matthew 6:34)

One more time, just in case we still don't get it, do not be anxious. This is probably the verse I remember the most when it comes to being anxious besides the simple and clear statement of "don't be anxious." Tomorrow will be anxious for itself; sufficient for the day is its own trouble. Tomorrow has enough issues and concerns all by itself, and I don't need to add to it. What I do need to do is be one of the people who keeps his eye on the prize. First Corinthians 9:24 states, "Do you not know that in a race all the runners run, but only one receives the prize? So run that you may obtain it." I want my prize to be an everlasting prize that comes from my heavenly Father. With that in mind, I will seek the kingdom of God and his righteousness. I will be ever growing in learning how to walk with the Holy Spirit to accomplish this goal. Galatians 5:16 states, "But I say, walk by the Spirit, and you will not gratify the desires of the flesh."

Questions:

1. Do you have the right prize out in front of you? Is the right prize motivating you?
2. How are you planning, working, training to win the prize you seek?
3. If you find yourself sidetracked, what can you do to get back on the track you want to be on, the track you know you should be on?

(Day 117)

Judge not, that you be not judged. (Matthew 7:1)

This is one of the most well-known and referenced verses in the Bible. Christians and pre-Christians both use it for various reasons. First Corinthians 5:12–13 states, "For what have I to do with judging outsiders? Is it not those inside the church whom you are to judge?" These two verses from 1 Corinthians 5 give us some clarity to what Jesus is telling us. Paul was the one speaking in 1 Corinthians, and Jesus was speaking in Matthew, but it is all the Word of God. Second Timothy 3:16 states, "All Scripture is breathed out by God and profitable for teaching, for reproof, for correction, and for training in righteousness." Scripture does not contradict itself and don't believe anyone who tells you otherwise. We need to show pre-Christians the love of Christ first, and then the Holy Spirit will convict them, while helping leads them into becoming more like Christ.

MATTHEW

Questions:

1. How familiar are you with 1 Corinthians 5:12–13? How could you (should you) apply it to your life?
2. When was the last time you considered 1 Corinthians 5:12–13 when it comes to judging (correcting, teaching) others?
3. When was the last time you considered the implications of 2 Timothy 3:16 on your life?

(Day 118)

> For with the judgment you pronounce you will be judged, and with the measure you use it will be measured to you. (Matthew 7:2)

What Christ is teaching is how we are to judge. The implication is that we will be judging, but there is a biblical way to do so. Making judgment on our brothers and sisters, those inside the church, is not to be light or flippant. To try and judge or correct others, you must be walking with Christ. Your judgment or correction must be guided from what is revealed in Scripture. To judge correctly, a person must know the revealed Word, be mature in their walk with Christ and walk with the Spirit. There is no room for hypocrisy here either. How you judge is how you will be judged. How you measure others is how you will be measured. Second Corinthians 13:14 states, "The grace of the Lord Jesus Christ and the love of God and the fellowship of the Holy Spirit be with you all."

Questions:

1. Do you walk cautiously when you are judging others?
2. Who do you measure yourself against? Where do you get your measuring stick from?

3. Would you feel comfortable and confident if God the Father was asking you to correct a fellow believer? Why or why not?

(Day 119)

> Why do you see the speck that is in your brother's eye, but you do not notice the log that is in your own eye? (Matthew 7:3)

These are two great questions from our Savior. They also bring into focus the importance of being humble when it comes to judging or correcting our fellow Christians. If we are not seeing the log(s) in our own eyes or not even recognizing the possibility of having a log in our own eye, it is due to being in wrong relationship with our Savior. We can all fall prey to the temptations of the enemy, and we must always be on our guard. I suggest the same thing when it comes to only noticing the speck that is in our brother's eye. We must cling to our Savior moment by moment, be in the Word, be in fellowship with other believers, and be constantly in prayer. Never forget who the enemy is (wolf), how he speaks (lies), and how he dresses himself (as a sheep).

Questions:

1. Are you aware of the possibility of having a log in your eye?
2. How do you prevent getting logs in your eyes?
3. Who would you go about removing a log from your eye?

(Day 120)

> Or how can you say to your brother, "Let me take the speck out of your eye," when there is the log in your own eye? (Matthew 7:4)

We are again seeing Jesus, using repetition to make his point. In back-to-back verses, he is suggesting that it is the person who is doing the judging that has the log in their eye when the other person only has a speck. Before trying to correct, guide, or judge another Christian, we better be somewhat aware of our own lives. Talking about how great you are is always more difficult than truly living it out. Usually, if you are great at something, people know it and will seek you out. Judging others is not an action to take lightly. Hopefully that is becoming clear in Christ's teaching. If you are not walking in obedience to Christ, how are you supposed to help others? Ephesians 4:1 states, "I therefore, a prisoner for the Lord, urge you to walk in a manner worthy of the calling to which you have been called."

Questions:

1. What are specific areas that you could work on when it comes to walking with Christ, living in obedience to Jesus?
2. Have you ever struggled with giving too much advice?
3. Is it easier for you to judge others or to work on your own walk with Christ?

(Day 121)

> You hypocrite, first take the log out of your own eye, and then you will see clearly to take the speck out of your brother's eye. (Matthew 7:5)

For three verses in a row, Jesus was using the example of a speck and log. In all three verses, the person with the log in their eye is the one who is approaching his brother or sister in Christ with the intent to judge or correct them. The person who is being approached is not facing as much chastisement from the true judge. Christ goes even further here and directly calls the one who thinks they are in right standing a hypocrite. This is not the first time we have read about Jesus calling people hypocrites, and it is never a positive title to receive. James 3:1 states, "Not many of you should become teachers, my brothers, for you know that we who teach will be judged with greater strictness." Biblically judging, correcting, and teaching others needs to be done with extreme reverence for the Word of God.

Questions:

1. What does the world teach us about becoming teachers and preachers of the Word of God?
2. How much fear does the world show when it comes to the judgment of God?
3. How is your church doing—the larger church doing—when it comes to hiring men to be teachers of God's Holy Word?

(Day 122)

> Do not give dogs what is holy, and do not throw your pearls before pigs, lest they trample them underfoot and turn to attack you. (Matthew 7:6)

Recall 1 Corinthians 5:12–13 that I referenced back when we were looking at Matthew 7:1. We have no business judging those outside the church. Those outside the church are not ready. They need to come to know Christ and his saving work. There is nothing wrong with asking someone if they have put their faith into the saving work of Christ, it will help you to know where they are in their journey. Many times, Christians are putting the cart before the horse. We are wanting people to look moral, to look like Christians, to act like Christians before they have even humbly come to Jesus in repentance and accepted him as the Christ. Giving to dogs what is holy, throwing your pearls before pigs, can lead to you being attacked. That is what Jesus is saying here. Know your audience. Are you in an edifying conversation or a salvation conversation?

MATTHEW

Questions:

1. Could our approach as Christians may be why at times we feel that we are being attacked? Is there a chance that we are doing things out of the order that God has given us?
2. When was the last time you had an edifying, God-honoring, Christian-growing conversation? What was the topic?
3. When was the last time you shared the gospel with someone, even just a little bit of the saving truth?

(Day 123)

> Ask and it will be given to you; seek and you will find; knock, and it will be opened to you. (Matthew 7:7)

Our heavenly Father likes and encourages us to bring our needs and wants to him, just like our earthly father does. That being said, we can't treat him like a magician that will grant our every wish on a whim. People are very emotional, and we can ask for things with wrong motives at the wrong time in the heat of the moment. Ask for things that might ultimately hurt us or even lead us away from our heavenly Father. John 14:13–14 states, "Whatever you ask in my name, this I will do, that the Father may be glorified in the Son. If you ask me anything in my name, I will do it." Everything we ask for is not in Jesus's name, even if we end our prayer with saying in Jesus's name. Asking in Jesus's name means asking something that is of his will. Can you imagine if everyone got everything they wanted? Thankfully, we serve an all-knowing God who gives everything at the perfect time. Our will and wants hopefully become conformed to our Savior's will as we continue to get to know him better each day.

Questions:

1. Does it bring you comfort knowing that our triune God knows which prayers are in our best interest?

2. Does it bring you comfort and/or wonder reading that the triune God wants to be in a personal relationship with you? He wants your company.
3. Are you seeking him for him or for what you hope he will do for you?

(Day 124)

> For everyone who asks receives, and the one who seeks finds, and to the one who knocks it will be opened. (Matthew 7:8)

Notice that the Scripture is telling us that if you ask, you will receive. Are we being told that we will receive exactly what we ask for? Remember, we are all fallen beings, and we don't necessarily know what we need. We will receive from our Lord what is best for the kingdom of God. Our heavenly Father does not make mistakes when it comes to giving to his followers. If someone is truly seeking the triune God and seeking to serve him with all their heart, mind, and soul, then they will indeed find what they are looking for. If a follower of Jesus Christ is knocking where Christ is directing them to knock, then the way will be opened. If the pre-Christian is knocking where Jesus is directing them, then that way will also be opened. The more we surrender to the will of our heavenly Father, or the more in-line we are with him, the more our prayers will be answered as we would like. The Lord's will, will be done.

Questions:

1. Do you find it easy to surrender to the will of your heavenly Father?
2. How do you turn from seeking what you should not be seeking?
3. Have you ever found yourself knocking on the wrong door?

MATTHEW

(Day 125)

> Or which one of you, if his son asks him for bread, will give him a stone? (Matthew 7:9)

As a parent of three boys, I do like to believe that I know them well enough to give them gifts that they will like. I also know that my wife and I will have the final say in what our boys will be receiving. Sometimes our kids ask for things that they are not ready for or for gifts that would simply be dangerous for them. I am not saying that they aren't asking for neat things, but certain gifts would not be a benefit for them and could even lead them to harm. As well as my wife and I know our kids, our heavenly Father knows each of his kids exponentially more. Doesn't it make sense that the triune God who created the universe will do a better job than human parents when it comes to giving gifts to his children? If we ask for bread, we can rest assure that he will be giving us the best bread possible and not a second-class loaf.

Questions:

1. Do you find it hard to accept the truth that your heavenly Father knows what's best for you?
2. What do you do when you feel like the triune God has given you a stone instead of bread?
3. How do you feel when someone you love feels like you have given them a stone even when you know it's what's best for them?

(Day 126)

> Or if he asks for a fish, will you give him a serpent. (Matthew 7:10)

Our heavenly Father will never give us a serpent, even if that is how we feel about the gift that he has given us. We might indeed not get exactly what we had asked for, but it most certainly will not be a gift that will harm us. Christ does not even tell us that he will have to explain his gift to us. We are to take the provided gift based on faith that our triune God does know what to give us and when he should give it. Luke 17:5 states, "The apostles said to the Lord, 'Increase our faith!'" If you feel like you could use a little boost in faith, you are in good company. The apostles themselves asked Jesus to increase their faith while they were walking with them. If those men were asking for increased faith, it is definitely okay and even encouraged that we ask the same of our Savior. Father God, help us to grow in our faith.

Questions:

1. Do you think you need help when it comes to being faithful?
2. Have you ever gone to prayer, asking your heavenly Father to increase your faith?
3. When was the last time you stepped out in faith?

(Day 127)

> If you then, who are evil, know how to give good gifts to your children, how much more will your Father who is in heaven give good things to those who ask him! (Matthew 7:11)

I love how often Jesus will break his lessons down into very simple statements. He is not suggesting that some of us are evil (fallen) but tells us that we are evil. Even though we are evil (fallen) we still know how to give good gifts to our children. I feel safe adding that we know how to give gifts to those that we love, in case you don't currently have children. He doesn't say that we give everything our children ask for, but we do know how to give gifts. So if an evil person even knows how to give a good gift, doesn't it make perfect sense that our Father in heaven will give us good things? He knows us better than anyone. He created us. He knows exactly what we need, even if we don't agree with him. All we need to do is to trust him, have faith that he does truly know what he is doing. For me, it is easier said than done. Thankfully, he is a patient and persistent Lord.

Questions:

1. What do you think when you read him addressing you as evil?
2. Where are you at when it comes to believing that he is giving you good gifts?
3. Where do you struggle most in not seeing his good gifts? To put it another way, what area(s) in your life do you think he could use some correction or guidance when it comes to giving you gifts?

(Day 128)

> So whatever you wish that others would do to you, do also to them, for this is the first law of the Prophets. (Matthew 7:12)

This is such an all-encompassing verse. Jesus has not placed any limit to location, venue, topic, time of your life or situation. He plainly tells us that whatever you wish that others would do to you, do also to them. Why is this such a struggle? If you don't think it's a struggle, read or watch the news for a moment. Humanity is constantly not following the golden rule, not following a very clearly stated rule. Numerous people—Christians, pre-Christians, you, and me—struggle when it comes to following this command. Can you imagine how beautiful this planet would be, how peaceful earth would be, if we could all follow this one teaching? Romans 7:15 states, "For I do not understand my own actions. For I do not do what I want, but I do the very thing I hate." Our battle with our flesh and temptation is real. What if we all asked the Holy Spirit to help us follow this one plainly stated rule every day?

Questions:

1. How do you do when you need to apologize for not following this command?
2. When are you most likely to not follow this command?
3. Where are you most likely to not follow this command?

(Day 129)

> Enter by the narrow gate. For the gate is wide and the way is easy that leads to destruction, and those who enter by it are many. (Matthew 7:13)

What a sad truth this is and I think one that is pretty easy to see. Take a good look at society, take a good look at our public schools seriously, go volunteer in your local public elementary school, and see what goes on in there. Hopefully, what Jesus is saying here brings you some sorrow and then moves you to action. It is not a statement to gloss over. Those who enter the wide gate that leads to destruction are many. We, those who have put their faith in the saving work of Jesus Christ, are not to enter through this wide gate but through the narrow gate. This is not to lead us to a defeatist mentality. We are still called and commanded to fulfill the Great Commission, and that is where our focus should be. Oh, how the world needs more strong biblically based, biblically founded, and Holy Spirit–dependent Christian leaders.

Questions:

1. How are you doing at avoiding the wide and easy gate?
2. Are you looking for the narrow gate or following the masses?
3. Are you actively trying to divert others away from the wide gate?

MATTHEW

(Day 130)

> For the gate is narrow and the way is hard that leads to life, and those who find it are few. (Matthew 7:14)

There is potential here to start feeling a little depressed after reading the last two verses, especially if we think we are the ones who actually save the lost. Do not think more of yourself than who you are. Do your part. Go and do. John 10:28–29 states, "I give them eternal life, and they will never perish, and no one will snatch them out of my hand. My Father, who has given them to me, is greater than all, and no one is able to snatch them out of the Father's hand." We do not give them eternal life, and we do not sustain the eternal life that is given by our heavenly Father. The triune God has blessed us to be ambassadors, messengers, and spreaders of the Word, but we do not actually save anyone. All glory to the triune God! Do not put more pressure on yourself than was intended, than what the Bible teaches us.

Questions:

1. How do you feel about the gate being narrow that leads to life?
2. How do you feel about the way being hard that leads to life?
3. Does this sound at all what the world teaches? The gate is narrow; the way is hard, and those who find it are few. There is only one source of truth.

(Day 131)

> Beware of false prophets, who come to you in sheep's clothing but inwardly are ravenous wolves. (Matthew 7:15)

Jesus is not talking about mean people but something worse. He is referring to people who are actively, purposefully trying to pull, direct, and lead the lost away from the truth. They aren't "just" blasting or mocking the Word but are teaching new lies, try to lead others astray by a different teaching altogether, creating a new belief system that contradicts the truth. They are also very good at what they do. Their camouflage is the best available; it is created by the father of lies, by the devil himself. They are not neutral but are being led by fallen angels, taught by demons. Luke 11:39 states, "And the Lord said to him, 'Now you Pharisees cleanse the outside of the cup and of the dish, but inside you are full of greed and wickedness.'" Romans 16:8, "For such persons do not serve our Lord Christ, but their own appetites, and by smooth talk and flattery they deceive the hearts of the naive." We must always be on our guard, staying dependent on our triune God and Word of Truth that he has provided for us.

Questions:

1. How aware are you of those out there looking to destroy you?
2. Should this cause us to live in fear (1 John 4:4)?
3. How serious are you when it comes to putting on the full armor of our God?

(Day 132)

> You will recognize them by their fruits. Are grapes gathered from thorn bushes, or figs from thistles. (Matthew 7:16)

Jesus is now giving us an analogy by talking about plants and what they produce. We know what different plants, trees, bushes, and general shrubbery are simply by looking at what they produce. If we can identify various types of plants just by recognizing what they produce, shouldn't we be able to do the same things with people? Everyone can be identified by what they are doing, what they put their time into, what their hobbies are, what they are passionate about, or what they invest in. People are recognized by their fruit. We are all drawn to different people by what we see them doing, what we perceive their interests to be, who we think they are, or by their fruit. Sometimes we may be wrong at first, which is why we need to truly take the time to get to know someone before we enter into any kind of lasting relationship or covenant with them. There is no doubt though; people are known by their fruit.

Questions:

1. What fruit do you look for in the people you surround yourself with?
2. How would people describe your fruit?
3. How long does it take to really know what kind of fruit people produce?

(Day 133)

> So, every healthy tree bears good fruit, but the diseased tree bears bad fruit. (Matthew 7:17)

How do we know what good fruit is? Where could we find some guidance in recognizing good fruit? Galatians 5:22–23 states, "But the fruit of the Spirit is love, joy, peace, patience, kindness, goodness, faithfulness, gentleness, self-control; against such things there is no law." I am so thankful that God gives us specific character traits to look for when we are searching for people who produce good fruit. Do we have any guidance when it comes to recognizing bad or diseased fruit? Galatians 5:19–21 states, "Now the works of the flesh are evident: sexual immorality, impurity, sensuality, idolatry, sorcery, enmity, strife, jealous, fits of anger, rivalries, dissensions, divisions, envy, drunkenness, orgies, and things like these. I warn you, as I warned you before, that those who do such things will not inherit the kingdom of God." Our flesh, our fallenness, is in direct opposition to the Spirit. Repent when we fail. Remember, our triune God is grace and mercy and ask the Holy Spirit to lead you and to help you walk in his ways.

Questions:

1. What does the world define as good fruit?
2. What are some worldly defined diseased or bad fruit?
3. How much do you rely on the Holy Spirit in your daily life?

(Day 134)

> A healthy tree cannot bear bad fruit, nor can a diseased tree bear good fruit. (Matthew 7:18)

For Christ's words to hold true, our definitions of good and bad must be defined by his Word that he has revealed, protected, and passed on to us. If we let other definitions of good and bad seep into our Lord's perfect definitions, then confusion and chaos will rule. We may see this confusion and chaos reigning supremely around the world, but we cannot succumb to it, promote it, or teach those that we love that it is correct (good) for how we will live our lives. To keep a strong defense, to live what is truly good and not become diseased, we must stay in the Word, be in fellowship with other true believers, be in constant prayer, and rely on the Holy Spirit to guide us and help us to walk in the truth. If we let our defenses down or become lackadaisical in our devotion to our triune God, then we will become fodder for the enemy.

Questions:

1. How are you keeping your defense strong?
2. How is your fruit looking today?
3. Where are you getting your fertilizer from?

(Day 135)

> Every tree that does not bear good fruit is cut down and thrown into the fire. (Matthew 7:19)

There is a refining fire that our heavenly Father puts his followers through for the benefit of his kingdom and for the benefit of his children. Hebrews 12:6 states, "For the Lord disciplines the one he loves, and chastises every son whom he receives." Christians will continually be refined until Christ returns as the conquering King or we are called home to heaven. There is also the real eternal fire where there will be gnashing of teeth. Revelation 20:10 states, "And the devil who had deceived them was thrown into the lake of fire and sulfur where the beast and the false prophets were, and they will be tormented day and night forever and ever." Luke 13:28 states, "In that place there will be weeping and gnashing of teeth, when you see Abraham and Isaac and Jacob and all the prophets in the kingdom of God but you yourself cast out."

Questions:

1. How important is it to you to bear good fruit? Where does it rank on your to-do list?
2. Do you embrace the Lord's discipline? How do you know if it is discipline from the Lord?
3. What do you believe about the place where there will be weeping and gnashing of teeth?

(Day 136)

> Thus you will recognize them by their fruits. (Matthew 7:20)

Our Lord and Savior, Jesus Christ, has made it crystal clear to us that the fruit a person produces is of utmost importance. Second Corinthians 6:14 states, "Do not be unequally yoked with unbelievers. For what partnership has righteousness with lawlessness? Or what fellowship has light with darkness?" Did Jesus ever talk, mingle, interact, and meet with pre-Christians? Of course he did; see John 1:1–11 for one very clear example out of many. Some might say, that's what he was constantly doing during his earthly ministry. Jesus could have stayed up in heaven and never interacted with people, but that is not what he chose to do. The fruit our triune God calls us to produce requires us to be out amongst the masses, but we are not to be yoked to them. Go and do, produce fruit as Christ and the apostles' role modeled for us to do, but don't become yoked to the diseased as you live in obedience to your heavenly Father.

Questions:

1. Who are you yoked to?
2. When do we read about Christ not being around people?
3. When was the last time you were out simply being with pre-Christians in a non-church event?

(Day 137)

> Not everyone who says to me Lord, Lord, will enter the kingdom of heaven, but the one who does the will of my Father who is in heaven. (Matthew 7:21)

We are seeing another example here of hypocrisy and how it does not produce the desired outcome. You can trick or mislead people with words. Some might define that as lying, but you will not trick the Lord God. Solely crying out "Lord, Lord," while living in unrepentant disobedience will not get people into heaven. James 1:22 states, "But be doers of the Word, and not hearers only, deceiving yourselves." What people say they believe should lead to action. If it doesn't lead to action, then they don't believe what they say. If you truly believe that you are a sinner condemned to eternity to hell, believe that Jesus is the Christ, repent of your sins, and ask him into

MATTHEW

your life. The only outcome is change (action/doing) in your life. If you don't truly believe the above sentence, then there won't be change, action, or doing.

Questions:

1. Does the Bible teach that you will be perfect after you accept Jesus as the Christ?
2. How is what you are saying lining up with your daily actions, your doings?
3. Where do we find or how do we know what the will of the Father is?

(Day 138)

> On that day many will say to me, "Lord, Lord did we not prophesy in your name, and cast out demons in your name, and do many mighty works in your name?" (Matthew 7:22)

In this verse, we see the opposite of what is happening in the prior verse. In this example, we read about people who seem to be doing the Lord's will, prophesying, casting out demons, and doing other mighty works in the Lord's name. Evidently, they weren't actually doing any of it in our Savior's name. They must have been doing it for their own glory. They must have been exercising their gifts in a hypocritical way, like what we read about in chapter 6. These people were focused on laying up treasure on earth instead of in heaven. Take a few minutes and reread Jesus's teaching on giving to the needy (Matthew 6:1–4), praying (Matthew 6:5–15), and fasting (Matthew 6:19–24). Do the work that our Father has called his followers to do, but we have to make sure to always give glory to the triune God. Acts 12:23 states, "Immediately an angel of the Lord struck him down, because he did not give God the glory, and he was eaten by worms and breathed his last."

Questions:

1. How do you do when it comes to being humble?
2. Is there an area in your life that you like to take all the credit for?
3. Do you believe there is a success in your life that the Holy Spirit is not enabling you?

(Day 139)

> And then will I declare to them, "I never knew you; depart from me, you workers of lawlessness." (Matthew 7:23)

This is one of the verses I remember the most and brings me some of the most sorrow and fear. What terrible and frightening words they would be to hear from the triune God while sitting on the bema seat. One of the most frequent prayers I pray for my kids is that the Lord will come to know my kids more and more every day and that he reveals more and more of himself to them every day. There is also an element of hypocrisy here on our part if those words are spoken about us. We must be honest with our Lord and Savior. There is no hiding anything from him, but he wants and desires that genuine, authentic, and true relationship with us. Relationships go both ways. Our heavenly Father has revealed himself to us. Do we go to him too, or is he always having to call us without us calling him back? He is *the* Lord, but he is more approachable than we can fully understand and always available.

Questions:

1. What do you imagine/vision when you read these words, "I never knew you; depart from me, you workers of lawlessness?"
2. Do these words motivate you? If so, motivate you to do what? If not, why not?

3. What would you like to hear when you face the final judgment?

(Day 140)

> Everyone then who hears these of mine and does them will be like a wise man who built his house on the rock. (Matthew 7:24)

I think and hope that we would all like to be considered wise in the eyes of the triune God. What greater compliment or accomplishment could there be then to hear our heavenly Father declare us as wise? He is the one and only judge that will matter when our time on earth comes to an end. Seek first his kingdom. A friend of mine is an impressive contractor, and I have had the opportunity to work for him during a few summers. What a visual I have of building on the rock (foundation) and how important it is. Make sure to be building your relationship with your heavenly Father on the Rock, there is only one rock. Hearing that leads to doing is a central piece of being firmly founded upon the rock. As we have read in prior verses, hearing alone or doing alone is not what our Lord wants. We must be hearers that move and grow into doing what we have heard from the triune God.

Questions:

1. How is your hearing, and who are you hearing from?
2. How frequently do you take time to hear?
3. How is your doing, and are you getting the correct directions before you start doing?

(Day 141)

> And the rains fell, and the floods came, and the winds blew and beat on that house, but it did not

fall, because it had been founded on the rock.
(Matthew 7:25)

There is no "if" mentioned here. The rains will fall, the floods will come, and the winds will definitely blow. You and those you love will be beat on. And the only thing stopping your house from falling will be where and how you built your foundation. First Peter 4:12 states, "Beloved, do not be surprised at the fiery trial when it comes upon you to test you, as though something strange were happening to you." Nothing unique is happening, and no one should be in shock when the fiery trials come—not if but when. The only thing each of us can do is prepare for the storms and trust in our Lord's sovereignty. Building our foundation on the truth that he has provided for us is the only way we will survive the coming squalls. There is only one rock that can hold together through each and every tempest.

Questions:

1. What types of storms have you faced, and how have you repelled them?
2. What types of storms do you fear the most? What storm is the hardest for you to stand against?
3. What storm do you fear might be out there waiting to strike?

(Day 142)

And everyone who hears these words of mine and
does not do them will be like a foolish man who
built his house on the sand. (Matthew 7:26)

There is one alternative mentioned to being a wise man and building your house upon the rock. A person could instead be a foolish man and build his house upon the sand. People don't set out to be foolish, but it does happen. Thankfully, those people can change course. Jesus has not told us that anyone has to remain a fool, repent, and change your ways. If you are finding that you are building your house upon the sand, stop! If you have already built your house on the sand, sell it or tear it down and begin to build a new house on the rock. Christ has opened the door, created the way for change, shown us the way to repent, and has made it possible for us to be seen as righteous before the Father. Foolishness and sand castles are the way of the world. Look to the truth and continue to build or start to build upon the rock.

Questions:

1. Where are you tempted to start adding some sand to the rock?
2. Are there influences in your life that are tempting you to mix sand in with the rock?
3. What should we do to continue to build on the rock or to start building on the rock?

(Day 143)

> And the rain fell, and the floods came, and the winds blew and beat against that house, and it fell, and great was the fall of it. (Matthew 7:27)

Remember the prior verse, Jesus is now telling us what will become of the house that is built upon the sand instead of the rock. Again, we read that the rain will come, floods will come, and winds will beat against us. If we build our house, our life, our worldview, and/or our belief system on the sand (the world), then not only will it all fall, but it will be a great fall. Sand castles can be fun to build with your family and/or friends on a sunny day at the beach, but they are not meant to withstand anything. A slight breeze can begin to erode a beautifully crafted sand castle. The simple splash from a harmless little wave can bring failure to the foundation, and a harmless swipe from a dog's tail can immediately cause a catastrophe. Be the wise man. Hear the words of the triune God, and do them. Build upon the one and only rock.

<u>Questions:</u>

1. How are you preparing for rain? Will your house leak?
2. How are you preparing for the floods? Will your house be washed away?
3. How are you preparing for the winds? Will your house be torn apart by the wind?

(Day 144)

> And when Jesus finished these sayings, the crowds were astonished at his teaching. (Matthew 7:28)

Never forget the crowds that came to listen to Jesus because they were astonished at his teaching. Luke 5:1–2 states, "On one occasion, while the crowd was pressing in on him to hear the Word of God, he was standing by the lake of Gennesaret." Getting into one of the boats, which was Simon's, he asked him to put out a little from the land. And he sat down and taught the people from the boat. The crowd was big enough that Jesus had to get into a boat to find somewhere to stand to teach. He would have done this out of necessity, not to show off; to build his brand; or to draw attention to himself. That isn't who Jesus is. The crowd was pressing in on him, so he found a solution to still be able to continue to teach him. Crowds also followed him wherever he went and stayed with him for extended periods of times, even to hunger (Mark 6:30–44; 8:1–10).

<u>Questions:</u>

1. When was the last time you felt astonished with Jesus's teaching?
2. How do you approach or prepare for Jesus's teaching?

3. Have you ever forgotten to eat or forgone eating to listen to the teaching of Jesus?

(Day 145)

> For he was teaching them as one who had authority, and not as their scribes. (Matthew 7:29)

Jesus's teaching had a recognizable authority. When he spoke, people knew that he deserved their complete attention. There was something different about this man from Nazareth, and it wasn't due to his carpenter skills. People were drawn to him, fascinated by him, and hopeful about who he could be. John 6:26 states, "And here he is, speaking openly, and they say nothing to him! Can it be that the authorities really know that this is the Christ?" They were so amazed, astounded, and bewildered by Jesus that they couldn't help but tell others about him. John 4:28–29 states, "So the woman left her water jar and went away into town and said to the people, 'Come, see a man who told me all that I ever did. Can this be the Christ?'" Mark 7:36 states, "And Jesus charged them to tell no one. But the more he charged them, the more zealously they proclaimed it." It was clear to everyone who heard him that he was different from their scribes. He was and still is something different. Jesus is the Christ!

Questions:

1. When was the last time you were moved, compelled to tell someone about Jesus Christ's teachings?
2. Do you believe his words have authority?
3. If they believed his words have authority, and if you call him the Christ, why is it such a challenge to obey his words?

ABOUT THE AUTHOR

Ryan R. Harder is an author who desires to encourage people to engage the Word of God, to come to know Jesus as the Christ, or to help the Christian come to know the triune God more each and every day. He has earned a BS with a major in biblical studies and a minor in intercultural studies, an MA in pastoral studies with an emphasis in family ministry, an MA with a double major in elementary and early childhood education, and an MEd in curriculum and instruction with a minor as a reading specialist. From time to time, he enjoys reading books written by C. H. Spurgeon, R. C. Sproul, Steven Lawson, John Piper, John MacArthur, and David S. Steele. Ryan has been married to his amazing wife since March 2005 and is blessed with three fantastic kids. He loves to be in the woods hunting, fishing, or riding four-wheelers with his wife and kids. Spending time with his wife and three boys is precious to him.